TO DAD ENJOY (
YOU ARE TO WE
BUS, LOVE SI

In the Wake of Giants

Journeys on the Barrow and the Grand Canal

TO DEREK
love Hon xx

Gerald Potterton

Now that you are sixty, its not so
much that you are over the hill, your
just further down the canal of life.

Have fun dad
and remember barge to port!
Love Ru x

BALLYHAY BOOKS

Published by Ballyhay Books,
an imprint of Laurel Cottage Ltd.
Donaghadee, N. Ireland 2008.
Copyrights Reserved.
© Text by Gerald Potterton 2008.
All rights reserved.
No part of this book may be reproduced
or stored on any media without the express
written permission of the publishers.
Printed by Gutenberg Press, Malta.

ISBN 978-1-900935-72-2

The Giants

❧

In the Wake of Giants is a somewhat obscure title that gives little clue to the content of this book. While it would be convenient to apportion the blame for this choice of title to another person, such as my publisher or my wife, I must confess that it is entirely my own choice. The theme of the book is centred on the Irish inland waterways. The adventure on which you are about to begin recounts my experiences and reflections as I travelled along the Grand Canal and River Barrow in a narrow boat. These escapades provided the ideal impetus to consider the work of the great civil engineers who designed these waterways and the labouring men who built them. Hence the giants referred to in the title are the engineers Thomas Omer, John Smeaton and the three Williams namely Jessop, Chapman and Dargan. Equally and very much included are the thousands of navvies whose names were never recorded.

However, the giants are not entirely confined to the eighteenth and nineteenth centuries. I also include a man whose lifetime has overlapped with my own. This man never lifted a pick or shovel, or laid stone carefully upon stone, or surveyed the course of a new canal through inhospitable terrain. But by his enduring written work he has ensured that the canals remained open for the pleasure craft of today. His name may not be familiar to all of you: L.T.C. Rolt is much better known to the English canal fraternity. All of these men with their individual and very different skills are the giants in whose wake I was honoured to travel.

*To my wife Olive,
for all her help
and support but
most of all for her
patience with me.*

Contents

1. The Seeds are Sown

∽

I can't recall when my interest in canals began. As a nipper I was always fascinated with feats of engineering whether railways, steamships, bridges or whatever. A black and white photograph hangs in our cloakroom of a rather glum looking boy with a group of adults gathered in front of a railway locomotive in full steam. While I do not appear to be enjoying myself, I suspect the problem was more to do with having to smile for the camera than a boring day out. The picture stems from about the early 1970s and was taken on a day trip with a steam preservation society. My father had more than a passing interest in such matters and so we were brought along. But while the rest of my generation were into the vinyl music of *Thin Lizzy*, Kawasaki motorbikes and cheesecloth shirts, all immersed in the unforgettable fragrance of Brut, my interests were of a much earlier era.

While railways have caught the imagination of many a young lad, canals did not generally hold the same appeal. There was no great noise or grandeur associated with water transport. There was none of the glory of a heavily loaded and smartly painted locomotive steaming through the night. Canals as a mode of transport were altogether gentler and less obtrusive. From a child's point of view, the canal is as dreary as a wet Sunday morning. But the experiences of our childhood can have a disproportionate effect on the rest of our lives. In common with many things in life, such an interest begins in a very innocent manner and gradually through an osmotic process you become more drawn in. Before you know it, you may be smitten. And probably some young people have slipped unwittingly into the murky world of addictive substances in a similarly naïve manner. In this regard I was better off with railways and canals.

As the Royal Canal is reasonably close to where I live, it was my enquiring mind on such matters that led me to explore its mysteries. It was also somewhere interesting to go for a quiet walk. Walking is, to my mind, one of life's great pleasures. However, being a farmer it's often not very relaxing to walk your own patch. The Sunday afternoon constitutional becomes reduced to a busman's holiday. You gaily set off with the best of intentions but invariably your mind becomes clogged up with management decisions, the majority of which it may be too late to implement. You return weary and uptight rather than refreshed and relaxed. Experience has told me that it's much better to take yourself off a short distance away. This also provides an opportunity to look across the hedges and reflect on other people's decisions.

Ideally walking should be done alone. A companion will only prove to be an unnecessary distraction. By walking alone your mind is free to take you where it will. How often has your thought process been entirely distracted by the pointless observation or interjection of your companion? Or your mind is a million miles away and your mate asks the most mundane question that has little relevance to anything, least of all to what you are thinking about. Now I understand that many a young man may have an ulterior motive in taking a walk of a Sunday's afternoon with the company of a young lady – and this can be fine and indeed honourable in itself. Equally it can be a very pleasant way to spend a few hours. I courted along the banks of the Royal Canal and I am bound to say that it worked out grand for me. But the two issues shouldn't be confused. Quality reflective walking that's intended to order your thoughts and ultimately clear your head should really be done alone.

Most of my canal bank walking has, for the latter reason, been solitary. Besides, once we were married my wife's interest in the Royal Canal, quite reasonably, went into steep decline. But born out of this walking habit is what I can only describe as a complete fascination with the beauty and accuracy of canal engineering. People who should know better tell me that I am in danger of becoming a canal anorak. My loosened and free mind wanders back to the late eighteenth century and the incredible human physical effort that was required to build these great waterways; human toil in sometimes the most appalling of conditions.

Water is the supreme judge of level and accurate work. The construction of roads and railways is a less exacting science; levels are not of paramount importance and inclines are tolerated. Canals have to be built as level as a billiard table for mile upon mile. Anyone who has ever put in a simple garden pond will be aware of this. Coping stones around the edge of the pond may appear to be level until the water is introduced. I recall complimenting a very professional gardener on how accurately his long and parallel ornamental still water features were constructed. It transpired that they were the work of a civil engineer hired specifically for the purpose. Everything else in the garden, he had done himself. Water is indeed a very unforgiving and exacting material to work with.

If my walk takes me under an arched road bridge, I always stop to admire the work of the stone mason and to offer him my respects. This humble man may well have not only cut and built the stonework but possibly designed the bridge as well. And stone, like water, is equally unforgiving. An ill-gauged blow of the mallet and many hours of patient work will fall to pieces, yet a single millimetre is enough to prevent the stone from slipping into place. But these beautiful natural products were cut to such geometrically difficult angles with the utmost precision. There is a superb example of a skew-arched bridge on the Royal Canal, near the Hill of Down, that is an absolute work of art. And yet it carries across its back, vehicle after vehicle, day in and day out with many of these loads exceeding its designed capacity by a factor of ten. Several of the early civil engineers began their careers as humble workmen. James Brindley, one of the pioneering canal engineers, started life as an illiterate farm labourer. Thomas Telford began his illustrious career as a stone mason and went on to build some of the greatest examples of bridge and canal engineering with just such a practical training. As my Sunday afternoon walk draws to a close, my mind will have come to its inescapable conclusion. I am firmly of the view that no matter what man chooses to build, it won't hold a candle to the work of the canal engineers and their civil engineering contractors.

To broaden our understanding of the magnitude of their work, consider for few moments the following scenario. Modern excavators are capable of moving a colossal amount of soil very quickly. With the help of a fleet of dump trucks, the landscape can be radically altered in a short time. Man's mechanical ingenuity over the last hundred years and fossil fuels make this possible. Precast concrete bridges can span long distances in a short period of time. It's all relatively simple and straightforward. Motorways can thus be quickly constructed provided, of course, that the chosen route offends no one.

Now, I wish to take you back a couple of hundred years. The intended route of the canal is surveyed and marked out. The great excavation begins with battalions of navvies – perhaps as many as 4000 men – armed with pick and shovel and the ubiquitous wheelbarrow. High ground is encountered and in order to avoid the cost of yet more locks, the waterway has to be cut around a hillside which entails massive excavation. Similar physical work is required to carry the canal on a great embankment across low-lying land. Absolute millions of cartloads of soil have to be piled endlessly on high. All of this supreme effort is carried out with human sweat, basic hand tools and an economical use of gunpowder. The end result is a billiard table level of waterway traversing every obstacle in its way. To my mind there is nothing to touch the greatness of this work and as an engineering project early canal construction remains virtually unsurpassed. The contemporary construction of the massive Three Gorges Dam on the Chinese Yangtse River is today's equivalent in terms of a conceptual plan and civil engineering on a truly grand scale.

There is another aspect to canal bank walking which is almost of equal importance to an appreciation of the engineering work involved.

Canals bisect the countryside between two given points. With no exceptions in this country, but with one or two in England, the chosen route will not be arrow-straight and entirely direct. For the canals essentially follow the contours thus avoiding, in so far as possible, very difficult terrain. And, not unlike today, the interests of local politicians and landowners were taken into account, sometimes resulting in a nonsensical route. Nor should we forget that the construction of the canal was potentially divisive. For many farmers it represented a major inconvenience. Fields and farms were carved in two and access was impeded. Drainage systems were changed and often complicated. The appearance of the surrounding countryside was altered.

Consider for a moment, the consequences of this construction for today's walker and canal user. It makes for a most interesting and often scenic route crossing the countryside in a haphazard manner.

No other form of travel can provide the walker with such an unrivalled perspective of the countryside. Canal bank walking or travelling on a boat will bring you to places that you never thought existed. In addition to this, the combination of water and secluded countryside will provide you with a unique insight into nature. It is the sum of these factors – the marriage of nature to early engineering that spawned my love of canals. But, while little did I know it at the time, there was another innate reason for my interest in these waterways. I will revert to this in a later chapter.

Sometimes in life an extraordinary sequence of events can happen. Several years ago in late summer I wandered into a second-hand bookshop in Athlone. My somewhat limited reading of canal based literature had, by then, extended to Ruth Delany's excellent book *Ireland's Inland Waterways* but that was about the extent of it. From my reading and re-reading this book, I recalled a reference to another, much older and out of print book entitled *Green and Silver*. But this was far from my mind as I perused the bookshelves, searching for nothing in particular. I then, rather bizarrely, spied an old hardback copy of *Green and Silver* and a quick flick through its pages suggested it could be a worthy purchase.

From that point on, I can safely say, my life would never be quite the same again. I very quickly became enthralled by this book. *Green and Silver* for those of you who may be unfamiliar with it, was first published in 1949. It is the account of a boat trip made by an Englishman, L.T.C. (Tom) Rolt, who set out from Athlone in a hired boat and travelled down the River Shannon to Shannon Harbour. There he entered the Grand Canal and proceeded up to Dublin. Leaving the city, he travelled on the Royal Canal up to the northern end of the River Shannon and eventually returned down to Athlone. The Royal Canal was closed to navigation shortly after he completed his trip. This very concise summary presents an overly simplistic view of what is a wonderful account of these waterways and of life in rural Ireland at that time. Tom Rolt had a wonderfully sharp mind and a great eye for detail. But the depth of his knowledge extended well beyond canal matters to all aspects of what is now referred to as industrial archaeology. Rolt's book was manna from heaven for me and was similar to a good appetiser that stimulates a latent desire for more to follow. I now needed to satisfy my growing appetite for more understanding and exploration of our inland waterways. However I should add that at that point in time that was all I knew about the author and the rest of his life was a complete mystery to me.

Now we must move on a few years, to the winter of 2004. In those days there was a biannual Smithfield Agricultural Show, held for hundreds of years in the City of London. It has since fallen prey to high city rents allied to a rapidly decreasing number of fulltime farmers. The show was a place of venerable pilgrimage for thousands of farmers, many of them Irish, to view the latest developments in agriculture. And I should add it goes without saying that the bright lights of London were an added attraction to this rural influx, many of whom may not have gotten out very often. I was one of these regular visitors. One of my sisters had an apartment in London at that time and naturally it provided the cheapest accommodation that we would find in town.

'I would like you to meet my new boyfriend,' Jill informed me over the breakfast, 'he's a nice fellow and I think you'll like him.'

My immediate reaction was that I had met so many of these 'nice fellows' that I couldn't care less if I never met another one. But as we were staying with Jill I decided it would not be polite or even prudent to articulate this opinion. I instead opted for a more muted response.

'Yeah, we'll catch up with you sometime,' I offered as a suitably vague reply.

'No, no, I thought we would go out to dinner tonight.' Jill, as ever, was very insistent.

Seeing that there wasn't going to be a whole lot of choice in the matter, I quickly conceded.

'OK, right, sure we'll meet up this evening,' I replied, trying hard to conceal a frown. The persistence of women, I thought, but there was nothing for it.

A posh Italian restaurant was duly booked by Jill – as the party was on me – and we all met up at the agreed time. I was seated beside the new man who was introduced to me as Peter.

I should point out at this stage that I have a slightly inquisitive mind and so I was determined to maximise the situation.

'So, what do you do with yourself, Peter?' I enquired. It's important to me that people are fully occupied. This had to be established first. His chosen occupation, that is if he had one, would probably determine the success of the evening ahead, or not.

'I am, I am a shipwright.' Peter replied, in his somewhat clipped English public school accent. It was also obvious that he was slightly thrown by the opening question.

I breathed a slight sigh of relief – this was promising enough. I would probably be able to engage this fellow in some degree of conversation. He could, after all, have been a fashion designer or an artist or a physiotherapist.

'So Peter, what sort of boats do you build?' I gently enquired.

'Wooden sailing boats, pilot cutters, fifty footers. Boats are in the blood. Matter of fact, I live on a boat.'

Peter, perhaps out of character, had clearly decided to put it up to me. Jill, in fairness, had probably warned him what to expect. Nonetheless, he had told me an awful lot in one short sentence.

'You live on a boat?' I echoed. 'Where, out at sea, in a harbour or a boat yard?' The possibilities were endless and to my simple mind each one was more ridiculous than the next. Fellow didn't even have a house and here he was getting serious with my sister. What would mother think?

'Falmouth, she's lying at anchor in Falmouth harbour. We take her out to sea at the weekends.'

'But you [singular] actually live on the boat, like all the time?' I persisted.

'I don't have a house, need a house, even want a house. Much better for the environment if more people lived on the water.'

'What, like in Thailand?' I questioned. But my mind was starting to become quite engaged. A thought crossed my mind.

'The only person I know of that lived on a boat was a countryman of yours back in the 1940s,' I added.

'On a narrow boat, then?' Peter needed further clarification.

I was taken aback by this.

'It was actually. He wrote a book about it and, matter of fact, it would be a good read for a fellow like you. His name was… …..' Peter interjected before I had time to finish the sentence.

'L.T.C. Rolt? He was a distant relative of mine,' Peter said with a proud grin.

'So what's your surname, Peter?'

'Rolt,' said Peter.

I was dumfounded. I was ecstatic. If Nelson Mandela had come into the restaurant and sat on one side of me and Jerry Hall on the other, I would not have been more pleased.

Peter and Jill became man and wife the following year.

2. What's in a Name

❦

There are times in life when you have to follow your instincts and go for it. I had toyed with the idea of buying a boat for some time. It was one of those niggling desires that won't give you a minute's peace until you deal positively with it. One afternoon, when crossing the Hill of Down Bridge, I spotted a narrow boat for sale on the Royal Canal below. I stopped to have a look – the mere action of walking around the boat was enough to help me realise how enthusiastic I was. My mind slipped back a dozen or so years.

When our eldest child was a toddler, along with two friends, we hired a cruiser on the Grand Canal at Robertstown, Co Kildare. It was Easter time and the weather was unusually cold and dry. We travelled down the Barrow Line and ended up below Vicarstown, where we moored for the night. One of my abiding memories is of waking up early the next morning and watching the mist rise off the water. It was a truly magical and unforgettable experience, not least because it was novel. With few exceptions, one tends to remember the first experiences of most things in life, whether for better or worse.

All of these fond memories came flooding back when I set foot on the Hill of Down boat. However, this was definitely not the boat for me to buy. It was, by no means, one of the finer examples of the craft of boat building. Unfortunately for those around me I am a particular sort of individual and I either take to something (or somebody), or not. My preference is always towards well engineered machines and this criterion was also applicable to boats. However the experience was useful. I knew that this boat thing was something I had to do. A trawl on the internet revealed a plethora of craft for sale. But it had to be a narrow boat. I had no desire for a fibre-glass cruiser that reflected my perceived status in the same way as many people choose their car. I wanted the real thing – an all steel traditional narrow boat designed and built for use on the canals.

It may be useful for some readers if I briefly outline the origins of the narrow boat. Essentially, these are craft that were originally built of wood with a beam of six foot ten inches and a flat bottom, to facilitate its passage in shallow water. The length of the boats varied anywhere between forty and seventy-two feet but the majority were closer to the maximum length. Originally built for the transport of coal on the British Bridgewater canal, within a short time narrow boats were used extensively for the carriage of most goods, whether in bagged, bulk or liquid form. The narrow beam was dictated by the restrictive width of the early canals, some of which entered very claustrophobic subterranean tunnels that led right to the coalface. On the stern end of the boat sat a small cabin to provide cramped living accommodation for the boatman and his family. This close-knit but deeply competitive community led a wandering life plying their cargoes protectively from one industrial centre to the next. There are parallels with the life of the modern truck driver; a high degree of comradeship intermingled with a jealous fervour over the entitlement to particular loads. With the demise in the 1950s of canal traffic and of this way of life, some of these boats were converted to full length cabins, entirely for leisure use. The subsequent growth in the leisure industry spawned a new generation of steel narrow boat builders. The uninitiated on boat matters might actually refer to these boats as barges (being flat bottomed) but the term narrow boat is more accurate. The stereotypic barge has a much wider beam. In the Irish context a (wide beam) barge is more typical as the narrow boat was never indigenous here; our transport needs were different and with the absence of tunnels the Irish waterways were of wider build than the early English ones.

Arguably, for the above reasons, the Irish canal purist should have a traditional Irish-style barge. Equally it could be said that I was too much under the influence of L.T.C. Rolt and the English tradition by wanting a narrow boat. To this accusation I must answer 'guilty as charged.' But neither will I deny the fact that a restored 1928 Vicker's built Irish barge with a Bolinder engine would be very desirable. However, I would want to defend myself by saying, firstly, I prefer the elegant style of a narrow boat. Secondly, such boats are practical; they can travel to places where wider barges are excluded because of their more obese nature. Thirdly, a narrow boat is all that I could afford without disposing of the family home, eating the dog and selling the children into slavery.

My search for a suitable boat was shortlisted to a few contenders, but one was head and shoulders above the rest. She was lying in Shannon Harbour, which is located in the great midland plains, close to the picturesque town of Banagher. I duly arranged a viewing and set off excitedly down the country one sunny day at the end of September 2006. Shannon Harbour is, in many ways, an interesting place with a great air of antiquity and former glory about it, being the terminus of the Grand Canal where it enters the mighty River Shannon. The old hotel building lies in a derelict state, as do most of the former warehouse buildings. In the harbour's heyday, in the first half of nineteenth century, the quays here were a hive of frenetic human activity. Passenger boats were arriving and departing here on a regular basis. Many of these people were reluctant travellers, bound for The New World via the Shannon down to Limerick. Meagre belongings were gathered together in an old flour sack containing the entire earthly possessions of some poor soul, departing the midlands of Ireland, never to set foot on Irish soil again.

Perhaps for me it is that human sadness that still pervades the air. However, on a more positive note Shannon Harbour was once an industrious centre of trade and transhipment. Ironically, given that the pangs of hunger were seldom far off, sacks of wheat and flour were loaded onto outward-bound boats, with potatoes, oats and cargoes of turf for the city. An excited shout from a ragged young lad would announce the imminent arrival of another boat with its Shire horse straining wearily on its harness. Nosebags were hung from the bit and bridle to allow the animal to feed while on the move but the bag was long licked empty of its oats by the end of the line. Many of the horses were provided by horse contractors while others were privately owned and became very faithful companions to the boat operator. Once uncoupled, the tired animal was led off to the stables for washing down followed by rest, while the fractious crew would shuffle into the local hostelries. The time for departure would come around soon enough for man and beast.

The talk in the inn could be heard out into the street, its flow and animation greatly helped by brimming jugs of porter. Arthur Guinness and St James' Gate were very important customers of the Grand Canal transport system and the boatmen reciprocated with the liberal consumption of their stout. News was eagerly exchanged; its spread was largely by word of mouth. Newspapers were the preserve of another class and these simple and hard working men were likely to be illiterate. And as these folk travelled more in a week than many of their fellow countrymen might have done in an entire lifetime, the locals would be keen to know what was happening in the next town and further afield. The conversation might have revolved around the new threat to the livelihood of these canal men – the railways were coming and would have engendered great fear as to the boatmen's future. Their concerns were not ill-founded for the glorious years of the canals were relatively short-lived. Shannon Harbour's days in the transport limelight would be over all too soon. The passenger boats were the first casualty to the iron road, which in turn quickly led to the closure of the hotel. But just as radio survived to carve out a lucrative existence alongside television, the canal boats battled successfully with the steam locomotive to carry a steady but declining burden of cargo for another hundred years or so. However, somewhat ironically, the Second World War generated a substantial upturn in the canal's twilight years as a result of the oil and coal scarcities. Ultimately it was the widespread adoption of road haulage in the post war years that signed the death warrant for the canals in these Islands. By the late 1950s the water ripples in Shannon Harbour were few and far between.

However, for all the decline of its glorious past, Shannon Harbour is once again a centre of boating activity. Its ancient quays bustle with the human traffic of the leisure boating industry. Its dry dock resonates to the sounds of angle grinders and hammers and the ultra bright arcs of electric welders as boats are repaired or refurbished. Mooring space is at a premium and on a good summer's day the lock is as busy as ever it was. Shannon Harbour is, in some ways, a parody of the modern Ireland in microcosm. Hard and relentless work but productive and fulfilling nonetheless, has been replaced with the more relaxed days of the lucrative leisure industry. The wheel has gone full circle; from a generation that knew no free time to a society that now spends more of its time and income in the pursuit of leisure than at work. It was in this Shannon Harbour that I found my boat.

If it wasn't quite love at first sight then it was something similar. The first time I set eyes on my future wife I knew she was the one for me. She didn't necessarily think so, but *sin scéal eile*. I am fortunate in this regard – I usually know what's right for me and then it's simply a matter of finding a way to achieve it. The narrow boat that lay in front of me now fell acutely into this category. This was, very definitely, the boat for me – she was beautiful. I accept that beauty is in the eye of the beholder but there is such a concept as universal beauty; in the manner that most men would fancy Jerry Hall, while a greater number would have more difficulty with the beauty of, say, Esther Rantzen. The former named beauty lay in front of me now, long and slender and elegant, with a natural radiance despite the fact that her makeup was a little tired. A little cosmetic bag-of-tricks would soon see to that. Now, I must stress that the analogy is discontinued when I tell you that I opened up her bow doors and had a peep inside. She was tastefully kitted out in light wood panelling and was surprisingly spacious with sleeping accommodation for four people. The galley was quaint with striking blue and yellow ceramic tiles around the sink area. An oil-fired cast iron stove up in the saloon created a very homely air. The master's cabin was in the stern. I knew that to sleep in this small cabin with its round portholes with the water lapping outside could only be a pleasant experience. The double bed was a bit on the short side – not long enough for the likes of Jerry Hall – but that was unlikely to be a problem and I'm not a very tall fellow.

I lifted the wooden cover on the engine bay. What greeted me was not the prettiest sight. It was, in fact, a greasy oily mess with the reek of dripping diesel. The engine, a marinised Ford diesel car unit, was second-hand when the boat was built in 1989. It was a tatty installation job but I tried not to let it blinker me about the rest of the boat. Nothing or nobody is perfect. It was something that I would have to sort out in due course.

I had seen enough to know that I wanted to buy the boat. But like the makings of all good deals, I didn't let on, as I love haggling. Practically anything that I purchase, I always try to get a decent reduction on the asking price. I fail to understand the words 'list price' or worse still, 'one price only'. The price of anything is only what you are prepared to pay for it. What the seller wants for it is entirely another matter. But I have to be honest here. Even if a seller asked of me a (reasonable) price that I thought was good value, I would still haggle. I always work on the maxim that every cent saved by haggling is much better in my pocket than in someone else's. You may think me an old(ish) skinflint, but I would choose to disagree. Money was scarce one time and it will be again. Anyhow, if you feel really bad or miserable about haggling you can always give the saved expenditure to a deserving charity. But do make sure that it is a deserving charity. And let me give you a word of warning. Haggling doesn't work everywhere. You have to be prepared to take verbal abuse and, if necessary, walk away. This is particularly galling when, although you really want to buy the item, you must leave it behind and walk away. Generally speaking, the posher the establishment the more uncomfortable they will be with this ancient practice. But one should still try. Don't let that put you off. Some years ago I was in Weirs, the jewellers, trying to buy something – I forget exactly what, it must have been some small present for my long-suffering wife – and the sales assistant started to gift wrap the item. I asked her then how much she really wanted for it;

'I am sorry, Sir,' came the puzzled reply.

'That price that's on the box' said I, pointing with an oily finger, 'no one in their right mind would pay that – bar an Arab.'

'I am sorry, Sir, but we don't give discounts,' she stuffily replied.

I started to write the cheque. 'You'll settle for a hundred less,' said I. You must always allow room for negotiation.

'Sir, I must insist on the full price,' my friend firmly replied, looking anxiously across at the security man.

'Look, as it's nearly Christmas, I'll split it with you,' I generously offered. But the poor girl was reared far from the language of the cattle trade and hadn't a clue what I was on about. I'd bet her father would understand, though.

'I beg your pardon, Sir, but I don't know what it is you wish to split but my instructions are that no discounts are allowed.'

'A half a loaf is better than no loaf,' I told her. But I knew I was beaten, the security man was taking an unhealthy interest in me and my wife had already deserted the ship. I had to walk away and without the partly wrapped intended present, mumbling under my breath that they'll want for money yet.

It would have practically killed me to walk away from this boat. But after a lot of theatrics, a price was eventually agreed on and I was now the very proud owner of a narrow boat. During the course of her life she had been encumbered with two or three awful names. The first, I can't remember, but at the time of purchase it was some silly cliché like *That's It Now*. It's almost as bad as naming a child Errol or Derrick or Concepta. While some would regard it as bad luck to rename a boat, I clearly had no choice.

Naming something that needs to be named is never easy. That said, there are certain no go areas, examples of which I have just given. As my wife and I have four children, each of which has two or three names, we have, by now, used up all possibilities and certainly anything that we like. As a matter of fact, by the time child number four arrived, we were quite run out of ideas. In the end, we got so frustrated in our search that I listed alphabetically about twenty christian names each beginning with a different letter of the alphabet, starting with the name Alison. We then had an election, whereby people who professed any sort of an interest could vote. But most of them were so fed up with the whole process that the poor child ended up with the first name on the list. She's Alison.

It's the same technique as the Irish electorate use when it comes to voting; we lethargically tick the first names that we come to on the ballot paper. A successful Irish politician's surname has to simply begin with either the letter A, B, C or D. That's why TD's Ahern, Brennan, Cowan and Dempsey always get elected. It's got nothing whatsoever to do with their ability. It's just that we couldn't be bothered reading down through the list. And who could blame us? However this does not explain as to how the TD, Leo Varadakar made it to the Dail. But maybe the electorate in his constituency use a different system and start at the bottom of the list, which would work equally well. Either way I'd say he really should change his name for the next time around by knocking off the letter V. And with a name like that it won't make any difference.

In the light of all this, naming the boat was not going to be easy. Learned people about such matters told me it should be a female name. This I had no difficulty with, but there was a sense of déjà-vu about it, as three of our children are female. Anyhow, I felt a good choice should not be limited by sex.

My mind was further afield. I wanted something unique – which is, of course, very risky – and ideally with a sense of history about it.

William Jessop was an English-born civil engineer who, whilst living a very quiet life, left some remarkable work after him. During his lifetime he carried out a substantial amount of very important work on the construction of the Grand Canal. His name is not hugely associated with this Irish work and has been almost forgotten. Hence I considered *The William Jessop*. My son greatly improved this to *Jessop's Step*, which was quite brilliant. It was, of course, for those of you who are not feeling quite so brilliant today, a double play on the word step. Locks are steps in the route of the canal and also as in following in his [Jessop's] footsteps.

There are of course several other great canal engineers, such as Thomas Omer, John Smeaton, and Richard Evans, all of whom worked in Ireland. None of these people caught my fancy in the same way. However, the supremo of these engineers has to be Thomas Telford but while he did visit Ireland and carried out some work on the harbour in Donaghadee, Co Down, he had no involvement with the construction of the Irish canals. Neither, did he particularly like this country and so, very regrettably, he too – for all these reasons – had to be disqualified. But he hasn't done too badly in the commemoration stakes having an entire English town named after him.

I then had a flash of genius. It doesn't happen half often enough but, though I say so myself, it's usually good when it does. My great hero of canal literature and preservation, how could he be overlooked? To ignore this man would be a missed opportunity. Maybe someone will have gotten there before me but so what? It was, of course, none other than the great L.T.C. (Tom) Rolt. I woke my wife up to share my brilliant inspiration (most of my ideas/schemes/strokes of genius come in the wee small hours) but she told me I was delirious and to go back to sleep.

Morning eventually arrived and un-deflated, I tried again. She was not for turning.

'So you think it's a pretty good idea, then?' I suggested, rather hopefully.

'What?' came the curt reply, in between buttering brown bread for school lunches. I should point out at this stage that my wife is not usually curt or even sharp. She has a very gentle and sweet nature, much, much nicer than me.

'The name for the boat?' I would see if she could remember my divine inspiration.

'You and your boat,' she replied with a pronounced hint of North of Ireland intonation. This is a sure sign that she's a wee bit flustered. 'Can you please go and feed the hens?' she asked. Maybe I should have quit then and waited for a better time. This would have been the sensible thing to do. But being an impatient, self obsessed male, I ploughed ahead.

'*The Tom Rolt*?' I offered.

'It's a ridiculous name. You can't call a boat something like that,' she replied grabbing a child (No. 4) and a half zipped school bag and rushing out the door.

Time is a great healer. Eventually, I garnered enough support with the widespread use of coercion and bribes. I was then given full and multilateral support. She was now officially *The Tom Rolt*. The naming ceremony would follow at a later date. However, I think I should have to justify my decision in arriving at this choice. To call a magnificent boat after an Englishman who wrote about canals and happened to be a relation of my brother-in-law was hardly reason in itself.

3. Green and Silver

෨

'I presume your boat is called after the great Tom Rolt?' questioned a man who was working on his boat, as I chugged past him in Lowtown, Co Kildare.

Lionel Thomas Caswall Rolt was born in Chester, England in 1910. He was born into a well-to-do family but, like many other families then and since, they were of mixed fortunes. One generation might add considerably to the family fortune, while the following one might be equally adept at depleting it. His father's tendency was more to the latter camp. Nonetheless, he got a good schooling but did not excel academically. From childhood he had been fixated with all things mechanical and his inclination was very much of a more practical nature. Consequently, his formal education finished (much to his delight) when he reached sixteen years of age. Largely due to the influence of his godfather, Kyrle Willans, it was agreed with his parents that he would serve an apprenticeship in mechanical engineering. Willans, who was an inventive entrepreneur – I imagine he was a bit like Commander Caracticius Pott in the 1960s film *Chitty*

Chitty Bang Bang – would become a very close friend and confidant. He was of the opinion that the young Rolt should learn his trade in the practical and time-honoured way.

The next five years were to become a very formative period in Rolt's life and I think, in many ways, made the man. He was now removed from the relative comfort of his public school and thrown into the steaming cauldron that was the workshop floor. He had exchanged the intellectual company of young gentlemen for the rough and raw men who judged character by a completely different set of values. Family and background counted for nothing; a man was judged by his physical strength and sharpness of eye. Men who could strike a punch with needle point accuracy. Men who could forge a perfectly round shaft out a block of iron, using only eye and hammer in perfect unison.

The young Rolt had much to learn. Initially clumsy in manner and in coordination, he was eager to succeed. The work on the factory floor of 1920s industrial England was relentless, the conditions poor and the hours long. In one memorable piece in his autobiography *Landscape with Machines* he tells of striking out iron rivets with a sledge hammer and punch inside the confines of a steam engine on an icy morning in December. His whole body would have taken a beating in such an environment, not least his hearing and his hands. His knuckles became raw from inexperienced and ill-gauged hammer blows. It was the toughest of schools. But for all of that, the more he progressed in his work the more he came to enjoy it. While Rolt initially found his fellow workers to be very rough and uncouth, he came to develop the utmost of respect for these men. He admired their skills, their tenacity, their integrity and their satisfaction in a job well done. These were men he would never forget. A bond was forged in these formative days that remained with him for his entire life. In his later years he would lament the passing of these traditional skills and the way of life that went with them.

At around this time, Willans bought a steam-powered narrow boat, *Cressy*, on which the family holidays would be taken. This was to become Rolt's introduction to the canal way of life. At weekends, he loved nothing more than to leave the heaving, smoking, smog-bound city behind him and travel down to Willans' home and potter around with the boat. Once his apprenticeship was served, he found that his skills were much in demand in the agricultural engineering sector. The era of the horse and steam on the farm was being rapidly overtaken by the diesel-engined tractor.

However there was time for other interests, as well. Despite being initially awkward and uneasy with the fairer sex, he developed into a charming and dashing young man with equally attractive young ladies never far from his elbow. It was a relationship with an adventurous, Irish born, young actress that spawned his interest in literature and writing – amongst other natural activities. It was she who introduced him to his life-long love of the poetry of W.B. Yeats. However love can be bitterly cruel and the very formative relationship was abruptly ended, leaving Rolt puzzled and a little shaken. But he was not alone for long and the void in his life was soon to be filled by another strong, attractive and challenging woman. Despite the formidable opposition of his intended's family, who were opposed to their wonderful daughter marrying 'a lowly mechanic', Tom and Angela Orred followed their hearts and quickly became man and wife. But even if not for this family, very turbulent times lay ahead for Great Britain and the rest of the world. Very shortly after the Rolts returned from their honeymoon, Neville Chamberlain announced to the nation that Britain was at war with Germany. Marriage can have an unsettling affect on some people and lead to a change of emphasis. Possibly due to this, Rolt's career started to change direction at this point. He became mildly frustrated with the path and pattern of his life and desired something quite different.

Rolt now made a courageous decision, which carried a high risk.

He would leave the security of his former way of life and begin travelling along England's great network of canals. Following an internal refit and the installation of a petrol engine, the narrow boat *Cressy* (which he had purchased from Willans) would become their marital home. His tools would be dropped from his hand and he would pick up the pen to provide his income. He, rather grandly, referred to his newly chosen lifestyle – which had the support and blessing of his new wife – as his Design for Living. Had this great turn around taken place ten years later in his life we might identify it today as a mid-life crisis. But he had become very disillusioned with life in the engineering industry and he longed for the open countryside which would allow him to develop his creativity in another way.

Thus his first published book, entitled *Narrow Boat*, was born out of this new itinerant life. It tells the story of life on the canals, as he saw it, in the England of the early 1940s. Strangely, there are few references within the book to the ongoing war, but their travels were halted during this period while Rolt spent the war years working for the Ministry of Supply. The book was to become a huge success and the fact that it is still in print sixty years later testifies to its enduring popularity. As to why it was so successful is less clear but tantamount to this was Rolt's ability as a writer. His enthusiasm for his subject was infectious. And the timing of the book's publication was probably very fortuitous. The Great British public were in transition from the austerity of war torn England to the new order that would culminate in the freedom of the 1960s. His newly chosen future looked to be very secure.

His book, *Green and Silver*, published in 1949, grew out of this success. It is, if you like, the Irish equivalent of *Narrow Boat*, and it too has become an enduring classic. It is a lighter, easier read than *Narrow Boat* in which book Rolt comes across as being very critical of industrial progress and the related growth of the sprawling suburbs. I find this to be somewhat ironic as Rolt was clearly fascinated with the Industrial Revolution and the associated development of canals and railways. In agriculture, whilst he was deeply interested in its hugely increasing mechanisation, he laments the demise of the traditional agricultural practices. But while his views were radical at the time, they are still relevant today.

For these reasons of dissimilarity, Rolt was attracted to Ireland, which at that time was a largely green and unspoilt land. There was very little manufacturing industry compared to his home country and agricultural progress was much slower. It is little wonder, therefore, that he became attached to this island of Yeats and slow reluctant change. Rolt was now at the pinnacle of his career as a writer. Book followed book, amongst which are his three timeless biographical masterpieces on the engineers Brunel, Stephenson and Telford, all of which are currently in print. But in tandem with his writing he channelled his extraordinary energy into his related interests of vintage cars and the preservation of steam railways.

By the time of his death in 1974, following an illness, L.T.C. Rolt had written over thirty books and countless articles. He died in his beloved house in rural Gloucestershire in the company of Sonia, his second wife and their two sons.

Undoubtedly, his pioneering work in rekindling interest in the inland waterways, both in Britain and Ireland, through his written work is his greatest legacy. And you must draw your own conclusions but his is the name that I feel honoured to commemorate on my humble boat.

4. The Maiden Voyage

❧

'So when are we going for a trip on the boat Dad?' youngest daughter (No.4) inquires. While she had been down on *The Tom Rolt* for a look, none of us had actually travelled anywhere.

'Next weekend is a bank holiday one, I'd say we'll all take off on the maiden voyage then,' I promised, sounding a bit like a father figure in an Enid Blyton story book.

Early on the Saturday morning of the October holiday weekend, we threw some sleeping bags and provisions into the jeep and travelled down to Shannon Harbour. My wife and a few sleepy stragglers stayed behind, to come down in a day or two. The plan was – in so far as we had one – that we would sail up the canal for a few miles, spend the night there and return to Shannon Harbour on the Sunday. We quickly loaded up our gear onto the boat and I apprehensively turned the ignition key to start the engine. It was clearly a case of beginner's luck. The engine fired up and with a shaky hand on the tiller, we set off up the canal.

The skill of steering a narrow boat is acquired quite quickly, provided everything is working with you and no one is looking. While you are steaming along a straight stretch, so long as you keep an eye on the bow, there's precious little to go wrong. But concentration is required and the tiller is a very unforgiving mechanism. If you deviate from your task for so much as a moment, you'll rapidly lose control and plough straight into the bank or another boat. However as a narrow boat is built like a battle ship, this is little cause for concern. Mooring at a jetty is the first real challenge to encounter. In an ideal world you would simply knock the propulsion lever out of gear and coast her in. But it's not quite that simple. If the propeller is not rotating, you have lost all positive steering action. You can pull and push the tiller handle every which way you like but rest assured, the boat will behave like a stubborn child and do the complete opposite. And once you get a narrow boat stuck crossways on the canal it takes a bit of sorting out. That said, we moored in to our first jetty in a reasonably acceptable manner. Yes, we broke a few cups when the bow gave the wooden jetty an over exuberant thump but the boat's brakes are non-existent and she weighs around ten tonnes.

Crew member No.1 was ordered to jump ashore, a line was awkwardly thrown across to him and the boat was safely moored. As we hadn't yet acquired a lock key and were absolute novices, it seemed prudent to phone for the services of a lock-keeper. He dutifully appeared and emptied the lock and then opened the gates for us to enter the chamber. I cautiously engaged forward, steered the boat out into the centre of the canal and set my sights on the centre of the lock. Once in the lock chamber, I retarded the boat by engaging reverse, she pulled up nicely and the lock-keeper set about his routine. I was pleased with my performance so far. The lower gates were then closed with their racks lowered to contain the incoming water. The land racks were then raised slowly with a torrent of water swelling up in the chamber and the level rising like a rapidly filling bath and lifting our boat. For beginners, like us, it's more than a bit scary and in a rising lock such as we were in the boat must be kept well secured to the wall of the lock chamber with lines around the mooring posts. The influx of water will cause the boat to surge forward if it is not well secured.

'I'll throw you up the rope,' I cockily called up to the lock-keeper. I had the rope coiled up in a manner that I thought John Wayne would have been proud of and I was trying very hard to look the consummate professional. My throw was awful, whereby I effectively lassoed the poor lock-keeper, causing him to stumble while the rope snaked back down towards me. But he managed to stamp on it with his foot and loop it around the mooring post and then handed the rope down to me. Clearly I was not the first poseur he had encountered.

'Where are yis headed?' he enquired, probably hoping that we had a one way passage to the Grand Canal Basin in the city, never to be seen again.

'Oh, we're only out for an overnight up as far as Belmont,' (a couple of km further upstream) I cordially informed him, 'we'll be back tomorrow.'

'What are you doing in that boat anyhow – did you buy it?' the lock-keeper enquired, 'cos that's Alan Crawford's boat.'

'Yeah, I did, I bought it off him,' I responded quickly with a sudden vision of the local Ban Garda peering down at me in the lock with handcuffs at the ready.

'Well,' he said, 'if that's the case you'd better get up as far as Tullamore.'

'Why's that?' I asked, sounding very puzzled.

'Cos you're only after buying the boat and this stretch of the canal is closing in a week's time until next March,' he said, adding 'you'd hardly want to be stuck down in Shannon Harbour until then.'

'Oh, I didn't know that at all,' I replied, full of righteous indignation as if the Minister of the Marine should have personally informed me.

'That's what's happening,' he assured me.

'How long will it take us to Tullamore?' I enquired.

'In that yoke,' he replied, pointing to the cloud of blue smoke billowing up out of the lock chamber, 'a good week.'

The former lock-keeper's cottage at Clononey was the subject of a television house restoration programme. Such a building provides a beautiful canvas to work with as these small houses have to be some of the most delightful places that anyone could wish to live in. With lovely proportions and often with a split level construction incorporated into the rising ground level at the lock, they are a joy to behold. But as any auctioneer will tell you the beauty of a property is often in its location. This is particularly true of these houses. Invariably situated beside a lock – with the sound of splashing water – and an idyllic vista outside your front door this is serenity personified. We would see many other very good examples of the craft of these house-builders on our travels, not least of which is the Round House at the 26th lock outside Tullamore. In that case the contractor got so carried away with building the lock-keeper's cottage to die for, that the directors of the Grand Canal refused to pay him the extra building costs incurred.

The 33rd lock at Belmont is a double lock, of which there are only a few on the entire canal system. But this one in particular is quite intimidating and difficult to work due to a road bridge crossing the lower chamber. For us it was similar to a jittery learner driver encountering the notorious Red Cow roundabout on Dublin's M50 on his first afternoon out. But Alan Wynne, the lock-keeper here, is a very professional guy and went out of his way to guide us safely through the process.

Belmont was a very industrious place in days of old. Perry's Mill is situated in a spectacular setting on the nearby River Brosna and the wharf just below the canal lock was a busy transhipment point for goods in and out. While the mill complex predates the construction of the canal, the coming of the canal to Belmont was hugely important to its success. The mill finally ceased operations some time ago but it is now open to the public and is well worth the short walk for a visit.

Many people – who have never set foot on a boat – have a poor understanding of the purpose for locks in a canal system. The popular misconception is that locks allow the water to defy gravity and for the canal to ascend and descend every hill and hummock in its path until it reaches its destination. There is a modicum of truth in this but in reality it is far from the case. It may be useful if we go back to basics for the moment. The purpose of a canal navigation is to provide a level (still) body of water at a constant depth for the passage of boats between two points. A river navigation may achieve the same objective, provided it is slow flowing, consistently deep enough and free of obstacles such as rocks, rapids and weirs. As outlined in the opening chapter, a canal is seldom the shortest route between two points for the following reason. In order that the body of water can be retained at a constant level for as long as possible – thus avoiding the use of locks (steps) – the engineer will have followed a convenient, albeit wandering, ground contour. Canals (with some exceptions) tend to go around obstacles rather than attempt to traverse them. However if it's not possible to avoid rising ground, this will have to be challenged head on. The canal rises in steps to this plateau – which becomes the summit level – and then the gradual unbroken descent to its terminus begins. Hence it's not (generally) correct to assume that a canal is continually rising and falling like the proverbial you-know-what. It is similar in profile to a stepped stile crossing a wire fence. And with one or two local mythical exceptions, water does not flow uphill – it will only rise to its own level. Therefore a good source of water, ideally a lake or river or both, is required to feed the canal on the summit level, and to compensate for the water lost at either end of the canal's route. The success of a good canal depends entirely upon it. In a dry summer, if the feeder source dries up then the canal becomes as useless as a pub with no beer. A reservoir may need to be constructed to guarantee this supply.

The Grand Canal system ascends to its summit level in Lowtown, Co Kildare where it is fed by two sources, namely the Pollardstown Fen and (formerly) the Blackwood Reservoir. From here it falls the entire way down to the River Shannon in the west and to the River Barrow in the south. Pollardstown not only has an abundance of water but it's also some of the clearest and purest in all creation. At the time of the canal's construction it was seen by the Dublin City authorities as a perfect supply channel for the city. Now in the twenty first century their avaricious eyes are set further west, on the River Shannon. The plan to use the canal source for the city was never implemented but Uncle Arthur Guinness recognised its potential and hence the canal water became a crucial component in the 'black stuff' for many years. You may well have heard a Dub use the expression that he was got well and truly 'locked' after ten pints of Guinness. While I won't claim to be an authority on such matters, it's entirely reasonable that the origin of this phrase is a reference to the source of the water in his favourite tipple.

There are enough locks for the beginner on this stretch of canal, as we travelled up towards Pullough, which in common with Lahinch and Rathmolyon and countless other places has several different spelling variants. The canal travels through quite a bleak and lonely landscape. On a warm summer afternoon with a cooling breeze blowing across the flatlands it would have much to commend it. But on a grey and foreboding evening in late October, it was difficult to get excited about. Anxious, therefore, to press on before nightfall, I pushed *The Tom Rolt* as fast as she would go. However, a narrow boat is no power boat – they are not built for speed. In fact, on many occasions, very purposeful and scary looking women, attired with ponytail, designer tracksuit, iPod and shades stressfully power-walk past me and quickly disappear off into the distance as I sail manfully along. But these ladies have my sympathy. The whole point of walking is to relax and to reflect and to tune into the sounds and scents of nature. But with the awful combination of headphones and Ray Bans and Dior all of the sensual beauties of the countryside that may be perceptible to these driven and tormented souls are well filtered out. I also fail to understand why sunglasses have become so indispensable to many people. They are a ridiculous fashion accessory as there are quite enough dull and depressing days in this country without diluting the benefits of some rare and precious brightness. But I console myself, did fashion ever make sense? I meet these scary ladies again on their return charge, knowing that they've allowed a few moments to pick at a low fat panini and sip a mocha in the village up ahead. I nod courteously passing some comment on the weather ever hopeful that it may initiate a conversation that could help me to understand their plight. But this has only met with very moderate success and I am little wiser. I press on unrequited and with a bit of luck and a tailwind I should reach the village in the next hour or so.

Daylight was to beat us and quickly draw the first day's travelling to a conclusion. We moored at the jetty below the 32nd lock. As we waited for the lock-keeper to arrive – this was a busy weekend as boats were coming in off the Shannon and travelling up the country – we decided to tie up for the night, once through the lock. The descending gloom was broken by the put-put of a small old cruiser-type boat, coming up behind us.

'Are youse going through the lock, or what?' came the unmistakable voice of a Dublin born boater, complete with denim jacket, moustache, hair like Pete Townsend of *The Who*, a gold earring and a couple of gold chains.

'We are but we haven't a lock key so we'll have to wait for the lock-keeper,' I responded, somewhat flatly.

'Jaysus, you wouldn't know when he'd appear,' he retorted, adding 'he's probably gone home – it's bleedin' dark.'

It was beside the fact that the lock-keeper lived more or less on the job. Our new acquaintance was clearly in no mood for hanging around.

'Have you a key?' I asked.

'Course I have a key,' he replied, 'I told you, you can't rely on them fellas.' This was, I felt, an unjustified damning indictment of lock-keepers. However, this was neither the time nor the place to correct this inaccuracy, bearing in mind that I was hardly qualified to speak, after just one day on the water. But my experience since tells me that this was, in fact, a grossly misleading generalisation. Most lock-keepers will go out of their way to help you.

'Throw us over the key and I'll put you through,' I instructed, adding the proviso, 'and then you can help us through.'

'Fair enough,' he replied and then shouted, 'here catch.'

We made plenty of silly mistakes like forgetting to close the bottom sluices before we started to fill the lock but eventually we got him – and his silent mot – up unto the next level. His boating experience transpired to be even less than ours. Thankfully the lock-keeper then arrived and put us through.

'Where are youse going to pull in for the night?' enquires our companion, 'jaysus, we're in the middle of the bleedin' bog here.'

While technically incorrect, it did sound like an accurate assessment of where we actually were. Ferbane was a couple of miles away and it is, undoubtedly, perilously close to the bog.

'We've little choice but to stop here,' I said, quietly coming to terms with the fact that this was the closest that I had ever slept to a Dub of this calibre, adding (to convince myself) 'sure we'll be grand.'

'Jaysus, I hope the savages around here stay in them trees over there and leave us alone. I'd never trust a culchie, particularly an Offaly one. Your man, Biffo Cowan, comes from down here,' replies our friend who obviously had similar neighbourly concerns to our own but for different reasons.

'Do you not like Mr Cowan?'

'I do in me bollocks. I can't stand any of them politicians. Bertie is the only one that you could rely on. The rest of them are a shower of ……'

'Hang on there a minute,' I interjected, 'what about Commissioner McCreevy and he the son of a lock-keeper up at Sallins? Do you not think it was him who fathered the Celtic Tiger?' I had no wish to defend our politicians but Charlie is in a different league.

'Celtic Tiger, me arse, he's on the way out now. He'll be dead and buried in the next six months. Mark my words.'

'Decko, will you shut your trap and tie this rope round the post,' roared his female friend from the stern of their craft.

'Aye, aye, Captain. Jaysus, you're in a desperate humour altogether.'

Decko disrespectfully drew his forefinger across his throat and quickly spun around to do as he was bidden. It seemed a pity that our conversation was so suddenly terminated, as it was becoming very promising.

The two boats were tied up, bow to stern. We switched on our battery powered lights and began to set up home. I set about lighting the diesel-fuelled stove in the saloon. The crew members began to prepare our first meal. It took an age before the stove was properly fired up and by then the fry was in the early stages of cremation on the pan. The tea was finally brewed and the three of us sat down – in much closer proximity than we usually do – to our supper. It was, as our first meal on the water, a new experience and the smell of the gas cooker combined with burnt sausages brought back memories of my childhood holidays stuck in a caravan in Clogherhead. All that was missing was the wretched gas mantles for light that blew up every time you banged the door. I reflected, with a mouth full of jammy batch bread, that I had absolutely hated caravan holidays as a child and yet here I was now back doing something similar. Confined, as we were, to a small space with no privacy, miserable light, poor sanitation facilities and somebody perpetually breathing down your neck. What was wrong with me or our house at home that I had resorted to this kind of activity? There'd be more comforts in solitary confinement in Port Laois. The children beside me were probably beginning to dislike it now almost as much as I did then. But rather bizarrely, all those years later, I was now really enjoying the experience. Age and adulthood can be strange; we seem to spend a lot of our lives trying to relive earlier years.

It was a good start to our first night on the water. The cabin was warm and cosy and we were very contentedly full, the washing up was out of the way and what more could a fellow want? But heaven on earth is usually very transitory. Happiness and general well being tend to very fleeting. One hopes that the eternal reward that we aspire to will be of a more permanent nature. All of a sudden and with no warning, the peace was shattered by the emanation from the stove of an unholy, massive stomach-type rumble. Had such a noise originated from a human being, it would have resulted in sudden death or, at the very least, a very obnoxious odour. The cabin was filled with fumes and we all started to cough and choke. I rushed up – in a manner that would make Red Adair look like a geriatric – and turned off the fuel, or so I thought. The flames went out and I threw open the bow doors. The smoke eventually cleared to the outside and we resigned ourselves to the fact that an early night was the only hope to keep warm.

'Sweet Jesus, what are youse up to? It's like Whiddy Island out here,' roared our companion as he emerged from his cosy little boat.

'The stove was acting up but it's out now.' I reassured him.

'Anyone burnt?' he asked with genuine concern. As is so often in life, it's never wise to judge people by their appearance or provenance.

'Ah no, it wasn't that bad.' I tried to allay our friend's fears.

'Thank God for that. I'd kill for a few scoops – will youse go halvers for a taxi into town? All that smoke has got me throat wicked dry.'

I have never been a big drinker, a pint or so of Guinness would keep me going for as long as I'd want. I've also been around long enough to know that to go into town with this man and his 'mot' would be the start of a session in which I would be totally lost. I would be puking like a baby by the time we were on the third round. George Best, when he was alive, or Liam Gallagher, could be hard pushed to keep up with my friend. But I had no wish to offend what was, after all, a decent and concerned man.

'I'd love to throw a few down my neck but the old ticker fluttered a month ago and I'm on medication. I can't drink anything because of the wretched stuff.' I lied, but I thought it was the lesser of two evils.

'Oh, that's a killer,' he replied. I was unsure whether he meant that it was the absence of alcohol or the heart disease that was going to get me.

'What about your man?' he added, looking at my long, gangly son who was all of sixteen years of age. I quickly answered on my son's behalf, desperate thoughts going through my mind.

'Oh, he'll be all right.'

'Heart as well?' my drinking companion questioned. He clearly had me sussed.

'No, that's OK so far as I know', I qualified.

'I'll see you in the morning then.'

'See you then,' I replied and added 'enjoy the evening'.

My friend clearly did enjoy the evening. I am a light sleeper at the best of times and the more so on the boat. I heard a car pull up and our friends got out. He was in the finest voice with a very rousing version of *A Nation Once Again*. I looked at my watch. It was 4.30am.

5. The Paris of the Midlands

✑

I awoke on Sunday morning, unsure of where I was but the slight rocking action of the boat quickly brought me to my senses. Looking around the wood panelled cabin with its single porthole on either side, I thought what a comfortable and pleasant little room it was. My focus was drawn to the engine which is boxed in at the foot of the bed. The decrepit old Ford was impossible to ignore. It had leaked enough diesel into the bilge yesterday to taint the cabin with a distinctive oily aroma. With a little time, I would sort the matter out. There were slight signs of life coming from the other crew members.

After breakfast, I was apprehensive that the engine wouldn't start, but it did finally splutter into life. But I had to resort to some robust motivational language to encourage it to co-operate. And in my frustration, I referred to the engine as if it were a living person, threatening it with all sorts of awful fates. It only occurred to me afterwards that our nearby boating neighbours may have thought I was verbally abusing one of the crew and that I did it all the time.

The canal crosses the Silver River via the Macartney aqueduct and is carried in a great sweeping embankment up to Derry Bridge. The parapet walls of the aqueduct are not built from cut stone but the finished article was deemed worthy enough to be named in honour of Sir John Macartney who was chairman of the Board of the Grand Canal Company. The Ringsend Docks were opened on 23rd April 1796 and shortly after, amid great pomp and ceremony, Macartney was knighted for his work on the canal.

While the intrinsic beauty of the countryside around here was not overtly obvious on this late October exodus, a subsequent return journey in early summer revealed this to be a secluded and very beautiful piece of creation. To refer to the countryside around Derry Bridge as the Garden of Eden would appear frivolous and excessive to most people but I have wonderful memories of an incredibly peaceful and unspoilt tract of meadowed countryside with its ancient castles in the background. But a location that can appear uniquely special in certain circumstances can be quite different on another occasion.

After passing through the Bord na Mona swing bridge we arrived in the attractive village of Pullough. In common with the aforementioned Belmont Mills, the coming of the canal was an important milestone in the history of this village. Once famous for its brickworks of which there were many in the locality, its distinctive soft yellow bricks were manufactured from a silty clay deposit and were moved by canal boat up the country. However, Pullough remains firmly in my memory for a particular reason. We were going along nice and steady and while the weather was on the cold side, it was at least dry. Suddenly the autumnal fragrances of the peat lands were overwhelmed by the unmistakeable smell of diesel. On reflection, there seems to have been no getting away from the oily stuff that weekend. I looked down into the water to check if we had ruptured the fuel tank on a submerged rock, or something similar. The water was reassuringly clear. I shook the rope on the brass bell – which my wife had given me and bears the inscription *Titanic* – to summon the crew members to the bridge.

'What's the smell of diesel?' I asked the Chief Engineer [aka daughter No.2] in a slightly belligerent fashion. She was, after all, meant to know about such things.

She didn't let me down. She knew.

'It's flowing out of the stove.'

'The what?' I queried, but I was pretty sure that I had heard correctly.

'The stove – remember last night?' questioned the Chief Engineer.

'Of course I do. Put down newspapers to soak it up, lift the mat, get the mop out and I'll pull in.' I was proud of my quick thinking under pressure. I should have been a divisional commander of the Irish Armed Forces out in Liberia – or the Lebanon. We quickly moored the boat and the diesel was, very definitely, flowing out of the wretched stove. I obviously hadn't turned the valve off properly after the incident last night. I knelt down and screwed the valve but it just kept stupidly turning and turning to no avail. And meanwhile the diesel siphoned out and unto the pine floor boards.

Now there are plenty of things which I am completely useless at, like cooking and hanging pictures and pruning roses. But for all of that – though I say so myself – I am pretty good with the spanners and welder. Most farmers are, with the exception of dairy farmers, who are hopeless. So, by extension, I should be well capable of turning a fuel valve off – if only it would turn off. It was clearly defective. In desperation and with rapidly mounting frustration, I attacked it with the vice-grip pliers and crinkled the wretched copper pipe closed. That sorted it, once and for all. We spent a good hour mopping up the diesel off the floor and then shoved all the oily papers into a bin in Pullough. The stove would be ceremoniously thrown out at the first opportunity. With vindictive relish I would have loved to fire it out there and then only it was much too heavy and awkward.

We had been on the water for twenty four hours by this time. With all factors considered it wasn't just quite as relaxing as I had planned and we were all becoming edgy and quite prickly with each other. Neither was there any way that we would be through Tullamore before dusk, that evening. Decisions had to be made. It would be best for all concerned to find a nearby safe mooring and leave the boat there until another fresh day. A perusal of the *Waterways Ireland* guide book found us what looked like being a suitable mooring. I rang the war office at home and my wife agreed to meet us at the 29th lock with a nice cheerful picnic of salad sandwiches. We'd make the tea on the boat.

Once across the Huband Aqueduct and passing by the ruined Ballycowan Castle, we arrived at the lock. The attractive surrounding countryside up here differs greatly from that which we had been travelling through since we departed Shannon Harbour. All that low lying pasture had started to get in on me; I needed some respite. The reassuring and undulating country up around Tullamore, with its more manicured hedgerows and mixed farms, all conspire to give a more managed and productive look. After a while the support unit arrived from home and we settled into a very pleasant picnic tea aboard *The Tom Rolt*. The drizzle that had started innocently enough as we left Pullough had, by now, progressed into a fully fledged wet evening. I spoke with the resident lady lock-keeper and she was glad to keep an eye on the boat until our return. With that we locked up and headed for home.

A week or so passed while *The Tom Rolt* lay at the 29th lock, just west of Tullamore. The maintenance-induced closure of this stretch of the canal was now only a few days away. I was anxious to move on up to the more unimpeded waterway at Ballycommon.

One of the problems of boating on a canal is that you require a crew. A minimum of two able-bodied people is necessary to skipper the boat and work the locks. However, if you are certain of having lock-keepers to assist you, arguably it is possible to manage single-handed.

But it's not entirely recommended as should a difficulty arise – as it invariably will – you will be a little short-staffed. This need of a crew can be a little frustrating, as I am essentially a solitary creature who is perfectly happy with just my own company. It goes with my occupation – farming has become a lonely business. Moreover, it's not everyone that I would choose to bring along for a day out on the water. Equally, I should add that there are probably a few people who would much prefer to spend a weekend in Mountjoy Jail, rather than be cooped up with me on a narrow boat. I like to think it's the boat that they have the problem with but this may not be altogether the case.

With a winter trip up to Ballycommon in the offing and with heavy lockage through a large town ahead, my usual crew were not exactly queuing up for the voyage. As a matter of fact, they were a bit rude about it. Like the story in the bible, they offered all sorts of feeble excuses. I was undeterred and I told them that I would go out and invite the waifs and strays (my friends) to come along. And, I added, they would be more than delighted to be asked. This threat failed to change their minds. I rang up Gerry – who is a like-minded sort of individual to me and a friend of long standing – and explained what I wanted to do. He said he would round up John, who is another sound fellow. A date was arranged and we duly set off for Ballycowan, on a frosty morning in November, stopping in Tullamore to buy the bread rolls and other necessary stuff for the lunch. As we left the town, Gerry spied a halting site for members of the unsettled community very close to the canal.

'Hey, young Potterton,' Gerry pipes up (he often refers to me in this somewhat disrespectful manner, at least in company but I let it go unchallenged as I rather like the young bit) 'see those fellows over there? I hope your old tub doesn't calve around here.' Now I must confess that this statement carries a suggestion of racism in it. But I doubt it was intended and I perceived that it was much more of a dig at me and my boat, rather than anyone else.

'Not at all, Gerry, there'll be no problem,' I reassured him.

We arrived at the boat and I tried to start the engine. It wouldn't go. We set up the jump leads and with the combined electrical power of two batteries and the three of us hurling every known threat at it, the engine decided it had better start. It spluttered shakily into life and then shamefully died a lingering death after about five revolutions. The next time it fired with a little more enthusiasm and mustered enough determination to stay running. As we moved off from the 29th lock Gerry and John were busy confabulating up in the bow of the boat. I could feel the slightest glow of heat from the November sun on my back. With the initial difficulties over, it would be a mighty day out. We moored the boat at the jetty to empty the 28th lock. I gave the trainee crew some instruction – if they would only listen, they'd be much easier to teach – but we got through without too much difficulty. I throttled up the engine and I could see a small crowd of people sitting on the bank up ahead, close to the railway bridge.

'Where's that steam coming from?' shouted Gerry. I saw it at exactly the same time.

'The engine, where else?' I replied in an irritated manner, annoyed as much by the question as the problem. I shut the engine down immediately and swung the tiller handle to try to bring the boat alongside the bank. There was a right boozy session in full swing close to where we were but fortunately on the far bank. I hasten to add that this undesirable collection of yobs was in no way connected to the people that Gerry had alluded to earlier.

'Gerry, hop ashore and I'll throw you a line. Pronto,' I commanded with all the authority of the late Charlie Haughey mooring his yacht at Inish Mhicelain.

'Who do you think I am, Eddie Macken on feckin' *Boomerang* at the water jump?' Gerry retorted in characteristic fashion. The boat was, in fairness, a good distance off the bank. Nonetheless, he made it to *terra firma*, and with no faults. A half full can of Lidl's cheapest came whizzing through the air and fell just short of its intended target, which was the back of Gerry's head. He kicked it into the canal in disgust. There were about twenty adult males in the group with enough shells at their disposal to take out a bunker in Afghanistan.

'How yis doin' lads?' I naïvely asked, not sure of what I was trying to achieve. There was no reply. Maybe they didn't understand.

I lifted the lid over the engine. It was not a pretty sight – the engine bay was half full of water. The alternator was even submerged. The prop shaft was splashing the water up and onto the exhaust manifold and this created the steamy sauna special effects. Everyone has a point at which they have had enough. I was rapidly approaching my point of despair. I felt almost like crying with desperation.

As a farmer, I have at my disposal quite a few agricultural machines, all of which are very capable of letting you down at the most inappropriate time. A combine that suddenly grinds to a halt, on the one good afternoon in a wet week, is particularly agonising. However, often the problem can be sorted by a phone call to the right person, who will know all there is to know about that particular piece of equipment. As a result, I have a list of contact numbers relevant to the key farm machines, stored in my mobile phone. In times of crisis these are the people I turn to and they are a true helpline in every sense of the word. Fortunately, as far as *The Tom Rolt* was concerned, I had recently added a new name and number to my phone. I would phone a friend – Justin. Justin knows about boats. He's also quite a character.

'Justin, it's me. I'm in a spot of bother.' No small talk, there wasn't time. The clock was ticking. The boat was in danger of going under. But Justin is one of those brilliant people who never gets excited in times of crisis and is virtually unflappable.

'Ah, the Meath farmer, what's the craic? Youse weren't any good in the football this year.'

While I greatly admire the attitude of such people they can, none-theless, try my patience particularly at times like this. Besides, I have no interest in football or hurling or rugby or any other sport.

'Justin, don't mind the football – the engine bay is full of water,' I said thinking I might shock him out of his very relaxed state.

'God, it's well for you to be out on the water, on a cracker of a day like this.' Justin was unperturbed. It was beside the fact that he was probably gone off into Galway for a day out with his missus. I decided on a change of tack.

'Justin, me and a couple of mates are out for the craic, but the arse of the boat is about two foot further down in the water than it should be.' It had the desired effect.

'Man, you got uno problemo,' Justin was serious now. 'Is the bilge pump not working?'

'Where's that Justin?' I innocently asked.

'Under the prop shaft.'

'Justin, I can't even see the prop shaft – it's under water,' I informed him.

'Did yis hit ice?' asked Justin, clearly reverting to his old self. It was a reference to my *Titanic* bell, which clearly hadn't gone unnoticed.

'Justin, I haven't the slightest idea where the water is coming in from,' I quickly responded.

'Have you saucepans and a bucket? Bail her out and check that there is power to the pump. If there's not, run a wire straight from the battery. Then get a seventeen spanner and give the two brass nuts on the stern tube gland a nip,' Justin instructed me, adding 'that'll sort you out and she won't sink. The steel bulkhead won't allow the water to get into the cabin. Give me a tinkle when you've that done.' I could hear the chink of glasses and voices in the background. I was right. A good lunch was obviously on its way.

'Justin, you're a saint (albeit an unlikely one), I'll give you a shout in a while,' I said, while pressing the red button on my phone.

I relayed the instructions to the crew. Gerry was still on the bank, holding the boat and keeping an eye on the yobs. But they were already too stoned to bother us anymore. They would be in a dangerous state by evening.

Two hours passed and by then our circumstances were greatly improved. The ingress of water had been stopped but the bilge pump was kaput. But we would manage without it for now and I steered out into the canal and headed into the town. I was tempted to moor at Bury Quay, beside the old bonded warehouse, which is now the home to the excellent Tullamore Dew Heritage Centre. But by now my crew were taking their roles very seriously and I decided there was a severe risk that they would feel obliged to follow the bargemen's time honoured tradition of drinking their heads off in Tullamore. It was now mid-afternoon and Ballycommon was still some way off. We kept moving and I returned to explore the town some days later.

* * * * * * * *

Tullamore is arguably the finest example of a canal town in Ireland. It is inextricably linked to the Grand Canal in what was to become a totally symbiotic relationship; each was completely dependent on the other. You can see an interesting clue to the town's past embossed on its metal street refuse bins today. It is the town's coat of arms which features a rising phoenix and there is an interesting story behind it.

In the 1700s, the Earls of Charleville owned everything around them, which included most of the town. By all accounts, they were not a bad lot and were pro development in Tullamore. The town was progressing along very nicely, until the reigning Earl was drowned while swimming in Ringsend, above all places. Today you'd probably be safe enough but in those days there wasn't any sewage treatment plants and the water quality must have something like Lough Sheelin in the 1980s. As to what possessed him to go in for a dip up there, history does not relate but his demise was certainly bad news for the town. His successor was a minor and so all further development and progress was frozen until he reached the age of consent. And to make matters worse, one summer's day in 1785, half of the town went up in flames as a result of a hot air balloon crash. A year earlier Catherine the Great of Russia had the good sense to ban balloon flights between March and December for this very reason. To this day, the people of Tullamore become panic-stricken when they see a hot air balloon in the vicinity. And I don't blame them. Sometime ago, one landed rather hurriedly beside me in a tinder dry harvest field. I don't think the old fellow who was flying it – or whatever one does with a balloon – had the slightest idea of the danger he posed to all around him. Besides, you would have to be either extremely laid back or very innocent to go up in one of those things, as God only knows where you will finish up. L.T.C. Rolt was fascinated by the early ballooning pioneers and his book *The Balloonists* is in print.

The phoenix was about to rise defiantly out of Tullamore's ashes. As is often the case, good fortune can follow on the coat tails of adversity. Several different factors were about to conspire together to ensure a great future for the town. The unfortunate fire gave the by now twenty one year old Earl a clean canvas to work with. He set about what was to become, in effect, a complete urban regeneration programme. His ambition was for Tullamore to become no less than The Paris of the Midlands. To help him achieve this, the Earl engaged the services of a property developer named Thomas Acres. This chap was to construction then what the firms of McNamara and Sisk are to the industry today. Between the Earl's money and Acres' ambitious schemes, they were set to transform the town. And let's face it, they had none of the hassle of planning permission or any of that sort of nonsense to get in their way. Like many of their modern day contemporaries they each built themselves trophy homes that reflected their self esteem. But in addition to the work of these two men, there was another reason why the town's continued development was entirely justified and sustainable. The Grand Canal was on its way to Tullamore.

The military engineer, Charles Vallancey – most of the early engineers were trained by the military, hence the term civil engineer arose as a reference to those who were not – was appointed to carry out a survey for the Commissioners of Inland Navigation. Included in his itinerary was a visit to Tullamore. The town's location was fortunate in two respects. Firstly it was close to the Commissioner's preferred route for the canal from the capital city to the lower River Shannon. Secondly, it was situated in an agriculturally prosperous area. Vallancey was firmly of the opinion that if such towns were serviced by the canal, the movement of food out of the area would be of a greater benefit to the wider economy. It was hardly macroeconomics, but large-scale inland commercial transport was a new concept. It should also go without saying that it's highly likely that the good Earl and his property developer friends exerted some undue influence on the Commissioners to ensure that the canal came to the town. After all, are not their modern day counterparts hugely influential as to the direction that the LUAS might take, or whatever? Major public infrastructural projects invariably create wealth in their wake and there is absolutely nothing new in this regard.

By 1798, the canal was cut as far as Tullamore. The importance of the canal to rural Ireland at that time cannot be over estimated. The roads were absolutely diabolical. Trade with the outside world was well nigh impossible and prohibitively expensive. The canal made it possible to move heavy loads with a fraction of the physical effort required to move them by road. In many cases a pair of horses was necessary to move a one tonne cart load by road. On the other hand, one horse was capable of towing a forty tonne cargo on water. The canal was arguably a greater revolution to commercial transport than the railway was to become. For slow travelling speeds, water is by far the most power efficient form of goods transport in terms of the motive effort required to move a given load.

Tullamore became the terminus of the Grand Canal for a period of five years. Just as there has been indecision and discontent about the chosen route of the M3 motorway at Tara, the canal's ultimate route from Tullamore to the Shannon was undecided for a few years. Thus, until the matter was resolved, a harbour with all the associated warehousing was required and so Tullamore built its first business park at that time.

By now the business ball was well and truly rolling. An influx of midlands-bound travellers created a need for a large hotel, which was rapidly built by the Acres consortia and open for business in 1801. The fly-boats (sometimes known as swift boats) followed sometime later which offered a fast, regular and luxurious mode of public transport with a twice daily passenger service to Dublin and Shannon Harbour. These boats were towed at speed by three trotting horses. At Shannon Harbour passengers could transfer to a Shannon steamer bound for Limerick or Ballinasloe. However despite the inherent speed advantages of the system, the fly-boats were not the revolution they might have been. The towpaths became very muddy and cut up in winter by the speeding horses and the canal banks were eroded by the increased wash from the boats. The coming of the railways was ultimately to seal their fate.

The early years of the nineteenth century were also very prosperous for agriculture, due to the stabilising effect of the Act of Union and the demands of the Napoleonic War years. A war economy is good for agriculture and this one was especially so; European grain imports into the huge English marketplace were practically non-existent. However when the Co Meath born, Duke of Wellington gave the French a good once and for all trouncing at Waterloo in 1815, this wartime agricultural boom should have come to an abrupt end. But in an effort to preserve the very lucrative farming *status quo* into peacetime, political pressure from the influential landowning legislature in Westminster led to the enactment of important Corn Laws in 1815. These laws imposed total restrictions and/or high tariffs on foreign grain imports into the United Kingdom of Great Britain and Ireland. This effectively guaranteed a continued high base price for domestic production. While these controversial laws were undoubtedly very beneficial to the (larger) farmers, their effect on the economy in general was much more contentious. Bread became more expensive in the cities and indeed, for some families, unattainable. Industry lost out due to higher wage costs and civil unrest. However, from Tullamore's trade point of view, these were prosperous times with boat loads of grain, potatoes and wool, along with local stone and brick, departing the harbour quays on a daily basis. Between 1826 and 1836, almost 13,000 tonnes of locally produced grain was transported annually from Tullamore up to the capital city.

The Grand Canal had reached Shannon Harbour by 1803. The now completed water transport link between Dublin and Limerick had a continuing positive effect on the town. Trade was to follow this corridor of water as surely as seagulls follow the plough. No longer would the great merchant trading families be confined to the port towns of Ireland. Tullamore, through its inland port, would give birth to its own hugely successful merchant and manufacturing class.

Distilling had had its roots set in Tullamore from before the arrival of the canal when, in 1829, Michael Molloy opened the distillery that would make the town synonymous with whiskey the world over. However it was the Williams family who were to become instrumental in developing the world renowned brand, Tullamore Dew. Tullamore was the perfect location for such an industry. High quality barley was locally grown, there was a ready labour force and the canal facilitated the efficient transport of the oak casks to the outside world. The Williams family were also to become a trading dynasty involved in the importation of wine, salt and tea, with twenty-six retail outlets across the midland counties. This business in much more recent times was to become, through a series of mergers and acquisitions, part of the Greencore PLC group of companies.

The Goodbody family was well known for its jute business with which it has long been associated with the town of Clara. However the family opened a cigarette factory in Tullamore in the 1820s and was an important employer in the town until operations ceased following a fire in 1886. The factory was then moved to new premises in Dublin. The firm of P.&H. Egan (whose name is still proudly emblazoned across a fine building) also evolved into a very significant merchant family. They later joined with the rival firm of Tarleton's, who were malsters, creating the firm of Egan Tarleton and Co. This business ceased trading in the 1970s.

All of these trading activities combined to ensure that Tullamore became one of the finest canal towns in the country. But as we have seen, many different factors came together to ensure that success. The coming of the canal did not guarantee prosperity to any town, but it often acted as the catalyst that allowed crucial development to happen.

6. Ballycommon Boy

❦

After *The Tom Rolt's* arrival in Ballycommon, she was to remain lying there for the winter. I had planned to move on up to Lowtown, but after spending a week or so in Ballycommon, I became very attached to this quaint place. In truth, there is not a lot there but it has a very rural, simplistic type of canal beauty about it. And the opportunities for retail therapy are limited here to its very old and unspoilt country pub, *Ballycommon House*, which as a hostelry predates the arrival of the canal. Ballycommon is also, of course, the junction at which the dewatered Kilbeggan Branch joins the main line. Jimmy, the lock-keeper, kept a watchful eye on the boat and I spent many quiet Saturday afternoons down there doing bits and pieces and generally pretending I was busy. There was plenty to do. I had planned on putting all the faults right and getting everything shipshape for the next season. The engine received a good service and the timing belt was changed. At this point I was intent on making a silk purse out of a sow's ear with regard to the engine. This was foolish and transpired to be a complete waste of money.

I knew that my family had a connection with Ballycommon but I had not previously been there or even knew where the place was. One could be forgiven for this as Ballycommon is hardly the centre of the Universe and is well hidden away from prying eyes. A couple of these relaxed Saturday afternoons were used to explore the link more fully. I will endeavour to keep this side of the story as short as possible, as I am fully aware that for an outsider, talking about one's children, relatives or dogs is as potentially boring as watching paint dry.

My grandfather was born into a Co Kildare family, close to the village of Carbury. This quiet backwater had been the family seat – if you'll forgive the rather ostentatious term – for a few previous generations. His father had done the sensible thing and married a woman not so much for her looks, but for her wealth. Thus, she (my great grandmother) came endowed with a house and, as they say, a farm of land in distant Ballycommon, Co Offaly. When their eldest son [my grandfather] came of age, his father sent him packing down to this farm. It got him out of his way which is always a good idea as father/son relationships can be stormy enough without actually trying to farm agreeably together. As an aside, I might add that most of my forebears seem to have been preoccupied with holding onto land and farming – often with only moderate success – to the detriment of any other career possibilities and everything else. And perhaps as a result we have precious few learned or even mildly distinguished ancestors. But while professional or clerical or military careers may not have been a priority, we've had a few shrewd operators and one ancestor in particular was a very astute businessman who, amongst other things, in 1886 founded the family auctioneering firm which continues to this day.

Arising from this, I have very little time for those people (related or not) whom I refer to as being soft option farmers, i.e. those who opt to farm principally because of peer pressure and are too lazy – or stupid – to consider doing anything else. Such people make the world's worst farmers, while they may have passed themselves as a barrister or a bus driver or some other profession that is more accommodating of serious ineptitude. However this was certainly not true of my grandfather as he proved to be an enormously capable individual at whatever he channelled his great energy into. While I never had the pleasure of meeting him, unfortunately he died suddenly a few weeks before my hasty arrival, I regard him as a giant in my own life.

My grandfather's exile to Ballycommon was in the early 1920s, which from an agricultural point of view, was preceding some very mixed years ahead. However if tillage crops were his forte – which they were not – the long-term outlook was good. Cattle production was much more uncertain, given that the Economic War with the United Kingdom was in the not too distant future. But as regards his farming in Ballycommon, the future was incidental for reasons that will become obvious later on.

Anyhow, grandfather knuckled down and got to work on the farm. His house was only a stone's throw from Chenevix Bridge in Ballycommon and the land ran down to the banks of the delightful Kilbeggan Branch line. This branch was sealed off from the Main Line in 1961 and thus became dry and neglected. But for all of that it is a beautiful 13km walk along the banks culminating in the restored harbour on the eastern side of Kilbeggan. The N6 dual carriageway crosses the dry canal bed close to the town with an elaborate contemporary bridge, which greatly facilitates the reopening of the canal should the funds become available. However this bridge is also very significant for another reason. A few years ago the authorities wouldn't have paid a blind bit of notice to the proponents of the disused canal or anyone else and have gleefully filled it in as if it never existed. Thankfully we have now moved on somewhat in this regard and this great modern bridge is certainly proof of that.

But we will now return to my grandfather living the carefree life of a bachelor down in sleepy Ballycommon. Just up the road and across a narrow accommodation bridge, which bears their family name, lived a farming family with a son and two daughters who were of marriageable age. This family, as we would say, kicked with the right foot, which was desperately important then. Inter-church marriages were frowned upon by both sides and all the more so in the early days of the Irish Free State. But it's amazing how things change. Now, as a parent, I will be happily relieved if the children get married at all whether it be to a Christian, Jew or Hindu, I am not that fussed.

Being a new young man in the area, it's likely he got an introduction to the family pretty quickly. Whether it was initially a matter of convenience or love at first sight, I can't tell you, but romance was soon in the air. And whatever their first feelings were towards each other it was, in the fullness of time, to blossom into a very successful marriage. I like to think that a large part of the courtship was conducted along the grassy banks of the canal, as I did the same myself. Being a bachelor man living away from home, he was probably invited over for the lunch on a Sunday afternoon. In an effort to spend some time together away from the inquisitive eyes of her father and family, his intended might have made a picnic tea and packed it up nicely in a wicker basket, fastened with straps. Throwing a tartan rug over his shoulder and picking up the basket, my grandfather would have respectfully enquired of his father-in-law to be, if it was permissible to take his daughter out for a walk. And in the early days of the courtship a chaperone was probably dispatched along with them, just in case, as this fellow was a blow-in from Kildare and you wouldn't know what he might get up to. But that was then. I very much doubt if any young suitors for my daughters will be as sensitive to my wishes. I'll probably be lucky if I get to interview them at all.

The walk would have taken them skipping across the tidy fields and down to the peaceful and secluded canal. Despite being a Sunday it's likely there was some boat traffic but not as much as on the weekdays.

And in that sense it was an interesting time for those who watched the passing boats. Many of the new steel diesel-engine versions were introduced in the late 1920s and probably caused quite a stir among the local canal communities. An idyllic little picnic spot would have been carefully chosen and the feast would begin with only the occasional clicking of a solitary grasshopper or a trout lazily breaking the surface to snatch a mayfly to distract them. With the picnic over and the crumbs shaken off the rug – to the delight of the watching robins – the couple might have succumbed to a little respectable bit of hows-your-father. And after a few of these occasions there was sufficient certainty for a marriage proposal to be offered and duly accepted.

My father was their second child and he was christened in the now ruined church in Ballycommon. But a move was in the air and fate was to take a peculiar turn. A distant childless relative up in Co. Meath – the astute gentleman mentioned earlier – bequeathed his house and farm to this young family. Whether they wanted to or not, they departed the small fields of Ballycommon for the plains of Co. Meath. Within a few years there would be no living family connection with this beautiful little spot. I was thus delighted to re-discover my connection with Ballycommon and the banks of the Grand Canal. While I could never claim to have come from a canal family who knows, maybe it is where the seeds of my interest and love of canals were sown.

On many occasions throughout the winter I would take *The Tom Rolt* out for a run up the canal to Daingean. This is a delightful and ever changing stretch of water, abundant in wildlife, not least with the frequent visits of the almost prehistoric looking heron. There are also swans along the way who would swim defiantly ahead of the boat and then tire of this escort work and return angrily to their patch.

Daingean is a pleasant small town, but it is an example of one in which the canal failed to change its fortunes to any great extent. It was once the county town but the progress of nearby Tullamore – as we have seen – usurped it and trade never developed to anything like the same extent. Between the 1600s and the 1920s the town was known as Philipstown but with the advent of the Irish Free State it reverted to its original name, which personally, I think a shame. Despite the fact that the name Philipstown might have too much of a colonial implication for some people – Philip of Spain and Mary Tudor were English Royalty – nonetheless it sounds a lot more attractive, to my mind. For this reason I was glad to see that a nearby house has not followed the trend and its name has retained the Spanish connection.

In April I decided that it was time to move on from Ballycommon. Spring was well and truly in the air and it was incredibly sunny for the time of the year. I vividly recollect lying on the warm coping stones at the mouth of the old Kilbeggan Branch line, painting *The Tom Rolt* just above the water line. But there are other sunny, secluded and peaceful little backwaters to explore and so, with reluctance, we left Ballycommon for the time being and set out for Edenderry.

It was not a particularly eventful journey, but one incident clearly springs to mind. We arrived at the Bord na Mona lifting bridge in the middle of the bog to find it down across the canal, thus blocking our passage. I went ashore but the bridge-keeper's cabin was locked up and the whole place was as desolate as Dingle in December. Neither was there sufficient room to turn the boat around. With visions of spending whole days and nights there awaiting the return of the missing bridge-keeper, I then had the bright idea of ringing Jimmy the lock-keeper in Ballycommon. Jimmy transpired to be an accomplished expert on this bridge and proceeded to instruct me over the phone while I pushed the buttons. The motors started to whir and gear wheels spun and with lots of creaking and groaning, the steel deck hinged upwards with all the inclination of a missile launcher. But there was a problem. I had become stranded on the wrong side of the canal, unable to get back to the boat on the other side to take her through. None of my crew on that day were seaworthy in this respect, either. It was a bit like the old riddle of the boatman with the fox, the goose and the bag of oats. Feeling incredibly stupid, I rang Jimmy again. He revealed that the bridge had, in fact, two sets of controls, one on either side. I had, of course, not seen the control box on the 'right' side and so had crossed over. Neither was I the first person to make this error. Jimmy instructed me to lower the bridge again and I marched back across the water with all the smugness of King Billy crossing the Boyne. I then proceeded to lift the bridge once more and then ran back to the boat and took her through.

From an agricultural point of view, this countryside is not particularly noteworthy, with a lot of the land in old pasture as it verges on the bog. But there are exceptions to this, with quite a few smart and tidy looking commercial farms scattered along the way. We moored up at Cartland Bridge – which is an attractive spot – and left the boat there for a week or so.

We departed our mooring on a very warm but showery Saturday afternoon in late April. Being a tillage farmer, the weather obviously plays a big part in my life – if not quite totally controlling it – but it's also an important aspect to the boater. As this narrow boat is steered in the open air with no protection from the elements whatsoever, a heavy shower will send you diving for cover. Warm summer rain is bearable but cold spring rain is deplorable. On such a day it's about one of the worst places on the planet to find yourself. Some cruiser-style narrow boats have removable tarpaulin covers fitted over the stern but there isn't sufficient room on *The Tom Rolt* for such a luxury.

Bright light is also important for an enjoyable trip; it can be difficult to get enthusiastic about anything on a dull cloudy day. It matters not a whit if it's freezing cold so long as there's plenty of Tyndall blue in the sky. Everything looks so much better when the sun is shining – and the more so on the canal – when you can see the trees and foliage perfectly reflected in the water. Sitting up in the bow on such a day, with the sound of water being parted by the passage of the boat is one of life's finer moments. With enough of a breeze to gently rustle the leaves and some cheerily optimistic bird song and a Mars bar chased down with strong tea, this is as good as it gets. If a fellow does not feel at peace with himself and his fellow man in such a situation, then regrettably he is in a bad way.

We had toyed with the idea of travelling down the branch line into Edenderry but a visit earlier that day had shown us that a large abandoned boat was practically blocking the passage, so we decided against it. But it's an attractive little harbour and is well worth a visit. However, it's difficult for me to get excited about this town and has that sort of midlands gloom mixed with the smell of turf smoke that pervades some of these communities close to the great tracts of bog. Notwithstanding, and in fairness to the town, great efforts have been made of late with large pedestrian areas and some very smart and brightly painted traditional-style shop fronts. But my failing to appreciate such a place may well be a peculiar weakness that I have in isolation. The agricultural land – some of it as good as you'll find anywhere in the country – that surrounds the bogland is also quite mundane and dreary. This may well come across as a snobby Co. Meath attitude and if it is, then I am betraying my roots.

7. Breaches in the Bog

❧

The Grand Canal from the Downshire Bridge at Edenderry to Ticknevin Bridge covers a distance of just over 7km. To many it may appear to be a rather exposed and uninspiring section of waterway. But nothing could be further from the truth. This stretch of canal is, possibly, one of the greatest feats of canal engineering in these islands. This may strike you as strange; it has none of the majesty of a grand aqueduct, it is not a deep cutting through rock, neither is it a great spine of embankment carrying the canal across a valley. It is none of these things. But the design and construction of this waterway, which skirts the northern edge of the Bog of Allen, was to defy some of the best engineers of the day. Thomas Omer, the Dutch engineer responsible for a lot of the earlier work on the canal, intended to take a direct route through the bog. While this may have appeared foolhardy, his methodology was plausible with the implementation of an extensive drainage plan prior to building the canal. However the directors of the canal board were not enamoured with his ideas, and they sought further advice. Word had trickled across the Irish Sea that the English engineer John Smeaton was an accomplished expert on all canal matters. He was duly contacted and he and his assistant, William Jessop, were persuaded to come over in the summer of 1773. Smeaton, being a much sought after and busy man, stayed here for a week or so, leaving Jessop behind to knuckle down and implement his ideas.

It is fascinating to pause for a moment and consider the difficulties of travel that faced these two men. As the age of rail was still a long way off, there were just two possible modes of transport up to Holyhead; either on horseback or perhaps by the nauseating and bone-shaking mail coach. The road to the port was diabolical, so much so that, after the 1801 Act of Union it became a bone of contention with the Irish Members of Parliament travelling over to Westminster. It was lobbying by one of these MPs, a Mr. Parnell from Tipperary, which ultimately led to the construction of Thomas Telford's great London to Holyhead road. It includes the masterpiece of early suspension bridge building, the Menai Bridge, which crosses from mainland Wales to the Isle of Anglesey. Such a major politically motivated road building project makes our own one-time TD and MEP, Mr P. Flynn's Castlebar by-pass look rather paltry by comparison. Commissioner Flynn might well have, by today's standards, delivered a six lane undersea and overland highway to the new hierarchical power, the Brussels parliament.

However our friends, Smeaton and Jessop, were of an earlier age and had a more epic journey to make. On eventually reaching Holyhead they boarded a sailing boat which – depending on the weather – would arrive in Kingstown (Dun Laoighaire) maybe a day or so later. By this stage they were exhausted, grubby and fed up with the whole sorry scheme that they had allowed themselves to be talked into. Neither would it be comforting to these busy men knowing that they were already the most of a week away from home and with nothing to show for it. From Kingstown, it's likely that one of the canal directors arranged for a hackney carriage to pick them up and bring them to their accommodation. A further day's hard driving was expedited to take them down to Edenderry. And whatever you may think of Edenderry now, it can't have been hectic then.

The final leg of their journey entailed a trek out into the middle of a bog... ......

I have included their travel itinerary for those of you who break into a cold sweat if you forget your mobile phone and become uncontactable for all of half an hour. Then imagine, if you will, a whole working week without being able to touch base. Or perhaps you complain about checking in two hours before your flight to London, despite the fact that you will be at your destination in under an hour after that. These poor guys had huge workloads to tend to with none of the transport and electronic communication facilities that we have at our disposal today. Our productivity should be correspondingly so much greater but despite their limitations these men achieved far more in their lifetimes than most of us can dream of. And while their work was in no way as physically demanding as that of the navvies within their charge, in reality they worked enormously long hours and were seldom at home with their wives and families.

Once on site, Mr Smeaton was not best pleased – to put it mildly – with the quality of work that he witnessed. You can imagine the scenario; he had spent precious time travelling here to be confronted with poor and shoddy workmanship even in the easier and more straightforward sections. He must have been horrified with the tardy efforts endeavouring to build a canal in a bottomless peaty mire. 'What in the Good Lord's name,' he pondered, 'was the daft Dutchman trying to achieve?' Radical action was called for and he quickly overturned Omer's plans and decided on the eventual route the canal was to take – along the northern perimeter. But for all his greatness, the English engineer was also on a steep learning curve and was not beyond making his own mistakes. He considered that the prior drainage of the bog was unnecessary and so opposed the thinking of both Omer and his fellow English engineer, William Chapman, in this regard. He directed that the canal be driven around the periphery and at the same level as the surrounding bog. This was reluctantly carried out by

Jessop who was well aware that this too was a recipe for disaster. The bogland effectively drained into the canal, causing it to shrink, thus leaving the canal raised and contained within embankments. But because these embankments were sitting on top of the boggy surface, they then slid silently away and the canal was breached. Weary with all of these efforts, William Jessop then decided to run with his own plans, which were a definite improvement. However, an extension of his thinking was to build a wall of clay behind the embankments to prevent them from pushing out even further. This was met with criticism and neither was it the perfect solution.

However, while occasional breaches were to occur at that time and indeed well into the future, Jessop's work was largely deemed to be a success. The canal today is a lasting testament to these engineers, including one John Killaly, whom we haven't mentioned. William Jessop was to remain the principal engineer to the canal board for many years. It is he who is credited with locating the summit water source, St James Well in Pollardstown Fen, and channelling it via the Milltown feeder to the summit level. A characteristic hallmark of all Jessop's canal work is meticulous attention to detail, ensuring that his canals have adequate water sources. To this end, with regard to the Grand Canal, he also constructed the Blackwood reservoir.

It would be an absolute injustice to the labouring men who dutifully carried out the engineer's plans, if we were not to consider their heroic work in terrible conditions. Spare a thought for the men – the navvies, so called because of their excavation work on the early inland navigations – who worked like Trojans in muck and water up to their knees for twelve hours a day. A skilled navvy at that time was capable of excavating twenty tonnes of soil out of a trench and up over his shoulder, day in, day out. The loaded wheelbarrows were pushed or winched up steep wooden ramps – the infamous barrow runs – and then emptied up to one hundred metres away. For longer distances, horse drawn wagons were filled by lines of labouring navvies and towed away along flat bottomed rails. Rock would have to be drilled – prior to blasting – with a pointed hexagonal steel chisel known as a jumper. This was skilfully driven into the ground by two sledge hammer wielding men striking in perfect unison while a third man held the jumper steady. Today you may still witness the same skill in split second timing demonstrated by circus men striking in the steel mooring pins for the big top. The explosive charge was rammed down into the chiselled hole and the fuse lit – very dangerous work. Relentless pressure from the gangers to speed up the progress, invariably led to horrific accidents. Men slipped and fell off the greasy planks of the steep barrow runs, perhaps left writhing with the pain of a splintered shin bone on the wet ground. Banks of soil were undermined in a cavalier manner to initiate a land slide to save time on excavation. The consequences were often perilous; men became trapped and were sometimes buried alive.

All of this supreme physical effort was often poorly sustained on a very basic and totally inadequate level of nutrition. These were big, giants of men – most of them over six feet tall – with a huge calorific requirement, the likes of which only a super heavyweight boxer would sensibly eat today. Ideally these men could usefully consume a couple of pounds of beef, a few loaves of bread and a flagon of ale per day. As for creature comforts, there were none. Living accommodation was on the work site, in draughty huts and outhouses, with just a few meagre handfuls of straw to ease the cold of the damp ground. The pay was poor recompense for the effort employed. However as these were an elite body of men, their wages were considerably higher than those of farm labourers. Away from their families for long periods, these men could return home to find a sick or bereft family. Old age came early and life was often brutally short.

Was there any happiness amongst these labouring giants? Did they derive pleasure from their work? How did they feel when the embankments of their labours shifted uneasily on the living sponge of the bog? Or, when they were sleeping, to be awoken by the sound of the restless bog rejecting all their efforts and reverting to its natural state? We can but guess the answers to these questions but suffice to say we live in a relative world. We, the people of today, do not possess anything like the same qualities of physical strength and mental stamina to endure a fraction of what they had to bear. But they knew no other life; they were conditioned to it from birth. Their expectations were low and their pleasures simple. They were a strong and resilient people unparalleled in the modern world.

If you ever have the pleasure of travelling along this great canal, spare a thought for these men and especially so as you travel across the Bog of Allen. Would they not be pleased to know that their glorious work remains in use for the purpose for which it was intended, two hundred and twenty years later? Nothing that I have done, or ever will do, can leave such a legacy.

Once you leave Ticknevin Bridge, the canal becomes quite twisted for a time and it's necessary to concentrate fully on steering the boat once more. The long level – which is 30km without a lock from Ballycommon to Ticknevin – and the straightness of the navigation as it crosses the bog, lulls you into a type of automatic pilot. It allows you plenty of opportunity to think and look around and to idly daydream. Once you become weary of this solitary state, you might liven things up a bit by starting an argument with the crew over politics or religion or some other such contentious issue.

As we came up to Bond Bridge, which is only a stone's throw from Allenwood, it was close to tea time. Once I become peckish, my normally pleasant enough demeanour changes to progressive degrees of irritability. As the hunger pangs become more frequent and acute, the smallest things start to annoy me, like the slightest vibration in the tiller handle or an obnoxious fly buzzing around my head. I then audibly threaten the wretched fly with all sorts of agonising and contorted deaths as he persists in lapping my head. But the scourge of an aggressive wasp is even worse; I fail to understand the mentality of such a creature whose sole aim in life is to inflict human pain and then fly away to certain death.

This was my state of mind as we approached Allenwood, so it seemed prudent to go ashore and stock up with some food. We are usually reasonably good about our diet on board but it won't be a four course meal with a sirloin roast (with Yorkshire pudding) or anything like that. But we have a few menu options, not least of which is a fry-up including brown bread, tomatoes and mushrooms. However the galley staff had allowed provisions to become low, so we walked into the small town to shop for our supper supplies.

In common with Oscar Wilde, I can resist anything but temptation. When you are hungry the smell of frying chips is one of the most heavenly scents known to man. Forget the scent of roses in late June, or newly mown hay in July or seaweed on Lahinch beach in August; the smell of chips frying in hot sunflower oil is unrivalled. We quickly tracked down the source of this aroma to a chip shop on the main street and immediately abandoned plans to prepare our own meal. Were we close to the sea, I would have opted for fresh cod but Allenwood is much too far inland for that. When in Rome, eat as the Romans do and burgers would be safer. While our order was being carefully prepared (we hoped), we decided to do a quick self-guided walking tour of Allenwood.

I have no reason to be rude about this Kildare town. With the exception of a clutch of gurriers gathered outside the chipper, in souped-up small cars – with rap music loud enough to waken the dead – I am quite sure the people of Allenwood are perfectly decent. But I find it difficult to become attached to this small town. Perhaps it is sufficient to say that, in common with Edenderry, an essentially linear town is always a challenge to beautify. For character, interest and charm, a town really needs to be endowed with a few ancient, narrow and winding streets and an old abbey or two. And it's difficult to stimulate interest in a town if it is not blessed with a river. Allenwood – through no fault of its own – has none of these necessities as it is not an old settlement. In its defence, I must record that the takeaway meal – which I was very happy to take away – was excellent. We dined on board and then weighed anchor and set sail for the short trip into Lowtown, where we settled down for the night.

Lowtown is a unique and very private place, not known to many outside the Grand Canal boating community. Even its name is an anomaly. Given that is situated just one lock below the summit level of the canal, it is to all intents and purposes at the highest point of the whole canal system. The coping stones on the 19th lock (Shannon Line) are 279.1 feet above sea level. Neither is it a town or even a village. Lowtown simply owes its very existence to the fact that the Main (Dublin) Line divides here into the (Waterford bound) Barrow Line and the (Limerick bound) Shannon Line. Such a location ensured that it was a place of great importance in the days of canal transport. But all of that is of a bygone era and there are but a few physical reminders left today of its illustrious past.

As we explored Lowtown on that April morning, I had a good feeling about the place. Lots and lots of boats are moored, bow to stern, of all descriptions and all ages. But I was delighted to see that I was in good company. There are, not unexpectedly, a greater collection of narrow boats and wide beams here than practically anywhere else in the country. Neither are there many big flashy cruisers. The boating fraternity in this quiet spot are the genuine article. These people love their boats, not so much for their beauty but as a way of life; in the same way as an old scruffy mongrel, who has served the family faithfully for decades, is loved and cherished. An outsider walking a designer poodle but knowing little or nothing about dogs cannot understand why they don't drown the awful creature and replace it with a new, desirable and well bred pet. That is not to suggest that the marina in Lowtown is home to a flotilla of scruffy old dogs – as it is not – but there are more cherished old floating family pets around here than you will find at, say, some of the Shannon marinas. But it all depends on who or what you are most comfortable with.

For the above reasons – and others – I was to become attached to Lowtown and it is a place I now know well. If you drive down to this small community on a cold winter evening you will smell the wood smoke from a dozen small stoves and see the soft yellow lights flickering on the water from the quiet and homely cabins within. These are a people who, for most of the time, live aboard and I find myself very drawn to their way of life. Many of their everyday needs are met in nearby Robertstown and there is a great pervading sense of a close, well-knit, community. But while I very much admire their chosen lifestyle, I don't think I could ever be fully part of it. Neither would it be very practicable for me to live aboard – for the time being anyhow.

What was the former coal yard in the glory days of the canal, is now the home of Lowtown Marina. New boats were built and hired out from here in the 1970s, but today boat repairs and refurbishments are at the nucleus of the activity. A crane service facilitates the lifting out of craft for painting or whatever else needs to be done. And in my somewhat limited experience of things nautical there are parallels between parenting a teenage family and owning a boat. Either the children or the boat are always in continual need of some item of expenditure, there's usually some teenage or boating crisis to follow another and, finally, they both can become very (ungratefully) time consuming. Perhaps if I were to follow the Shannon example, and owned a new shiny state-of-the-art craft, such a parallel might not exist but that wouldn't solve the difficulties and concerns of the parenting issue. Anyhow, as the mind of a worrier hates to be idle, I would undoubtedly conceive new and greater worries to fill the vacuum. And are not most things in life transient and fleeting? Time and effort and financial input are usually rewarded, provided, of course, that the money and effort has been sensibly spent in the first place.

While we strolled around the Marina on that first April morning, I found what was to be an unlikely treasure trove. In what was originally built as the old sugar store, in which sacks of Carlow sugar awaiting transhipment to the city were stored, is now home to a quaint chandlery. The character of the establishment is apparent before you enter the premises. The door is a reclaimed oak affair complete with square wooden dowels, more appropriate to a medieval castle. Opening this door emits an eerie creaking sound that Boris Karloff would have killed for in one of his horror movies. A large pot-bellied stove stands to greet you warmly of a cold spring morning. The minimally lit shop is long and narrow and is stocked floor to ceiling with most, if not everything, you could ever need for a boat. The proprietor is a forthright lady with a distinguished accent, quite different to the native version as heard in Allenwood and district. Both she and her husband are an absolute fund of knowledge on anything nautical. As I looked around me, I was like a child waking up on Christmas morning and sneaking a look at what Santa Claus had left at the end of my bed. There were plenty of things that I needed, not least a wood burning stove and fenders and a boathook and paint and a bilge pump…... the list went on and on. With a moderate degree of restraint I gradually ticked everything off the list, at least until the following weekend.

As you will appreciate by now, I have spent a considerable amount of time in Lowtown. It has, certainly for the present, become my home port. Consequently, I am frequently in and out through the 19th lock and have come to know Jimmy Conroy, the lock-keeper reasonably well. In our early conversations, it quickly became obvious to me that Jimmy was an expert on canal matters. I tactfully told him so, to which his reply was;

'You want to hear my mother.'

It was an opportunity that was too good to miss.

8. Bring us back a Parrot

⚮

Jimmy Conroy is the fifth successive member of his family to keep the 19th lock at Lowtown. This, surprising as it may seem, is not a record in itself. Alan Lindley is an eighth generation lock-keeper down at the 30th lock, in Rahan. Conroy's family, on his maternal side, have lived beside the lock and worked the racks here since 1872. His great grandfather was one Murtagh Murphy, who was the first of his family to live at Lowtown. But Murphy's predecessors were connected with the Grand Canal since its inception.

There is a great air of antiquity surrounding the original lock-keeper's cottage, in which Jimmy Conroy's mother was born and still resides in today. The building dates from the construction of the canal in the late 1700s and now bears a slate roof. The original roof was thatched but the marauding Black and Tans – a renegade unit of the British Army – torched the roof during the War of Independence. They did so, on the pretence that the cottage was hiding a volunteer who, presumably, they wanted to interview. The occupants of the cottage were not hiding anyone and the wanted man duly emerged, wet and bedraggled, from a nearby culvert once the soldiers had moved on. It was also interesting to note that the lady I was about to visit was born a few short years after this acrimonious period in Irish history.

We were shown into the small and comfortable parlour, just as the November light was fading, to reminisce about life on the banks of the Grand Canal. I knew I was in for a memorable evening. In the small window, through which the vision of innumerable boats had passed, sat a low wooden table neatly laid with a lace cloth. Centred on the table was a simple cross. But even if this overt sign of a house of deep faith was not there, I would have sensed that generations of a devout family had lived here safe in the knowledge that, no matter what, they were within God's care. In my childhood, practically every rural house that one might visit had a religious relic or picture, given pride of place on the kitchen wall. Nowadays the tradition is regrettably confined to the traditional homesteads of a rapidly disappearing generation. The island of saints and scholars in the twenty first century has new idols for veneration, many of which can be bought and sold. The low wallpapered walls of the parlour – which had heard so many conversations over the centuries – were hung with several photographs of canal interest. Many of these were taken when the camera was in its infancy. On the settee a couple of lever arch files lay open, crammed full of pictures and newspaper cuttings – anything and everything to do with the canal. It was indeed a privilege and an honour to be invited in to such surroundings and converse with a quite remarkable lady.

Mrs Esther Conroy (Essie) was born in the room where we now sat. Her father (Thomas Murphy) was the lock-keeper here from 1918 until 1939. In those distant days, Essie was keen to impress upon me, the life of the lock-keeper was particularly hard. My mind immediately flashed back to the days of my grandfather, down in Ballycommon – he may well have known this man. Lock keeping then entailed a twenty-four hour day for the full seven days a week with only an hour allowed off for Mass on a Sunday. The canal boats – they were never referred to as barges – were moving at all hours of the day and night. The fall of darkness did not bring any respite, boat travel continued throughout the night and with practically no lighting. How the skippers saw where they were going is difficult for us to understand but they obviously developed a sort of sixth sense. But accidents did happen. On a dark winter's night, the boat No. 41M was involved in a head-on collision with 53M near Shannon Harbour. Neither boat was showing any light. At that time the arches of the bridges were painted white to allow them to stand out on a moonless night. And painting the ends of the lock balance beams and the mooring posts the traditional contrasting black and white colours also helped in this regard.

As a result of this perpetual motion on the waterways, when Thomas Murphy heard a boat put-putting up towards his lock in the middle of the night, he had to forsake the comfort of his bed. Throwing an old sack over his shoulders, he quietly left the heat of his hearth to set the lock. And woes betide him if he failed to hear a boat. But there was little fear of that. Not only would he hear the boat at some distance away, he would instantly indentify the boat by the distinctive sound of its engine. The skipper would expect the lock to be ready for him to sail straight into, without so much as slowing down. And this is understandable. In common with the lock-keeper, he did not particularly relish his job in the wee small hours of the night. Furthermore, he was anxious to press on to his ultimate destination.

In these hours of darkness, when hand signals would be to no avail, the lock-keeper would signal to the oncoming boat by striking two matches. This informed the skipper that he was out of his bed and was about his job. When the lock was ready he would give the all clear, by striking three matches. The boat would begin to enter the lock chamber and the next few minutes were critical to both the skipper and the lock-keeper. Nor should we lose sight of the fact that the entire operation was carried out in the paltry glow of a Hurricane lamp. For the uninitiated, who have never had the pleasure of setting foot on a boat, barge or yacht, call it what you will, it's important to understand that none of these vessels can be quickly retarded. A boat is brought to a halt by shifting its propeller into reverse. Thus you hear that the huge container ships must engage reverse thrust about 4 km out from port to avoid demolishing all before them. An unretarded canal boat would be less horrific but nonetheless, with a gross weight of around sixty-five tonnes, capable of serious destruction. However, on these old canal boats it was only possible to reverse the propeller by stopping and restarting the engine, which was a major job in itself. It wasn't just a matter of simply turning an ignition key. It took fire and elbow grease to excite these single cylinder semi-diesel monsters back into life. Nothing short of Divine intervention would persuade the skipper to slow the passage of his boat by killing the engine and engaging reverse. It was the responsibility of the lock-keeper to bring the boat to a rest.

If I may digress for a moment, I happen to own a vintage tractor with a very similar sort of engine to these early Bolinder diesels, as were first fitted in the canal boats from 1911. These engines are, in effect, a cross between a steam engine – where combustion takes place outside of the cylinder – and the internal combustion engine, as we know it today. To start my Fowler engine you will need a box of matches and several small pieces of ignition paper soaked in saltpetre and a big burly fellow with the biceps of Mike Tyson. The lit paper is placed in a special receiver and screwed rapidly into the cylinder head. The four litre capacity, single cylinder monster is then heroically cranked over with a three foot long iron handle, ever fearful that the engine might backfire. If it does, the starting handle will be ejected with the velocity of a surface to air missile. It's entirely possible that it will break either your arm or leg or, if you are the really unlucky sort, both of them together. If this method fails to get her running – or if you can't find a big burly and Red Bull fuelled Tyson type – there is another approved starting option. You carefully place a special explosive cartridge (similar to a shotgun cartridge but without the pellets) into a breach on the cylinder head. Then, wielding a hammer, you firmly strike the detonation pin. If the cartridge explodes – as it should – it will send the single cylinder spinning into life and you are off for a nostalgic run. If the cartridge fails to detonate, you have a few problems. Firstly, the engine has not started and secondly, but much more importantly, you are left with a primed unexploded shell to deal with. If you happen to know General Sir John de la Chastelaine's number, give him a tinkle and he'll be well able to talk you through decommissioning it. If not, try the Irish Army Bomb Disposal Unit, office hours only. Either way, you won't be doing much with the tractor for a day or two. However, probably wisely, the canal boat's Bolinder engines did not have this engine starting option.

You will, by now, understand fully why the skipper chose to rely upon the lock-keeper to retard the boat in the lock. But what follows is a critical and potentially dangerous task. A stop rope was thrown from the boat as she entered the lock, which was deftly caught by the lock-keeper. He hitched this around the stop post in a special manner, to bring the boat to a gradual but positive halt. If a running hitch was not used the momentum of the boat would be sufficient to break the unrelenting rope and the bow would impact the deep gate with terminal consequences. Equally, in a rising lock the bow could ram the sill with a very destructive thud. Therefore, it was of extreme importance that the lock-keeper got it right, and halted the moving boat in the correct, progressive manner, or damage would invariably occur. And it goes without saying that it was all too easy for the lock-keeper to lose his fingers as the rope tensioned. In our conversation,

Essie told of an incident whereby an inexperienced lock-keeper had his ankle severed in such a manner by the stop rope. Once the boat was safely moored in the lock, the rudder was turned across the stern to keep it from fouling on the sill or the gate planks. It was expected that the whole process should be done and dusted with the boat on its way again in a mere fifteen minutes.

When Thomas Murphy died in 1939, his son, Thomas Junior – who was Essie Conroy's brother – was eighteen years of age. This was most unfortunate, as ridiculous as it may seem, the Grand Canal Company would not employ anyone under the age of twenty five years as a lock-keeper. Despite the family's protests, the Company evicted them, lock stock and barrel from the lock-keeper's cottage. Faced with nowhere to live, in the hungry 1930s, the now desolate Mrs Murphy returned with her family to her own people. The only accommodation that was available to her was an old barn in the farmyard, where the family lived for the next six months. But being of resilient stock, Mrs Murphy continued to fight her corner with the canal authorities. A compromise was arrived at whereby the family was allowed to return to the cottage, provided that Mrs Murphy supervised her son until he was twenty five years of age. It was an unbelievable situation that depicts the canal authorities in a very bureaucratic and dispassionate light.

However, conditions for canal people were to improve somewhat by 1946, when the working day was reduced to sixteen hours. But the pay was still dismal, even by the standards of the time, at the equivalent in today's terms of €3 per week. The house and small garden were included, as was turf for the fire but for all of that the lock-keepers were not particularly well treated by the Grand Canal Company. They lived in dread of some of the company's inspectors, who were likely to cycle up the towpath at any time and nitpick over some irrelevant trivia. Failure to comply with their often petty requests made the lock-keeper's life very difficult. Equally working and maintaining the lock was by no means a lock-keeper's only chore. There was much more to the position than simply that.

As the 19th(S) lock is a summit lock, through which the entire Shannon Line is watered, control of the water level by the lock-keeper is vitally important. In addition to this, canal water was formerly extracted downstream by both the ESB for the cooling tower in Allenwood power station and Bord na Mona in Lullymore. The lock-keeper had to allow for this water loss and still provide sufficient to maintain the levels down the canal. Equally, the extravagant or excessive use of water being allowed through a rack – whether intentionally or not – was a cardinal sin, which incurred the wrath of the inspectors. A measurement of water levels had to be recorded on a daily basis. In a previous chapter we have noted that the Guinness Brewery in St James' Gate used the crystal clear water from the canal as a vital ingredient in their porter. This water was extracted at the 9th lock in Clondalkin. And Uncle Arthur was very fussy about the quality of the canal water. To this end two inspectors were dispatched to the 19th lock every Monday morning, without fail, to sample the water and note its cleanliness. We must remember that at this time – unlike today – the canal was kept in pristine condition. It was dredged on a regular basis, the banks were kept free of vegetation and the water weeds were laboriously cut. And it is also reassuring to know that there were no on-board toilets discharging into the canal at that time. That said, if the Guinness inspectors saw anything untoward floating in the canal, there would be an almighty fuss kicked up. Arthur Guinness and Co ceased to use canal water in the 1970s.

In addition to his lock and water level duties, the keeper of the 19th lock had other special responsibilities to tend to. The company boats were refuelled here, while in the empty lock, from a large gravity discharge oil storage tank. The boat's fuel tank was dipped before and after filling and the fuel use recorded. The oil line still extrudes from the chamber wall but the tank was removed some years ago. Because Lowtown was a transhipment quay with the off and on-loading of cargoes, the lock-keeper monitored the boat movements and their cargoes. Let us assume a boat – we'll say it is 42M – departed St James' Gate at 6.00am, laden with fifty tonnes of porter, in barrels and firkins. By 10.00pm that night, 42M would have travelled the 41km to reach Lowtown. This equates to almost 3km per hour, including the time taken to pass through the nineteen locks. It's hardly a record speed for goods transport, certainly by today's standards, when we can't wait more than a couple of hours for anything. But we mustn't lose sight of the fact that the boat's cargo was the weight equivalent to that carried today by two large articulated trucks. Two such trucks would have a combined power of at least 800hp. Our friend on 42M had 15hp. That considered, he was doing pretty well. Thomas Murphy Jnr would have heard 42M spluttering down from Robertstown and had the lock full and ready. The boat was loaded to capacity and sitting so low in the water that in the skipper's words, 'a mouse could drink off the deck'. While in the lock, Murphy informed the skipper that there is a change in plan and that the porter must be offloaded on the quay forthwith – as it's destined for Limerick – and the boat is to be reloaded with bagged sugar and return to the city. Rowntree's sweet factory in Islandbridge were in a panic for the sugar. Needless to say the skipper would not be skipping with delight when he heard this news. But such was the life of a boatman and he wearily moored his vessel to the quay.

To ensure that the cargo was the same weight as was despatched from Guinness' that morning, the lock-keeper read the effective weight of the boat by recording its draught on its depth gauge. He then compared it to the dispatch docket. Counting the barrels was not accurate enough, as some of the porter might have been drawn off by some thirsty poor soul on the way down to Lowtown. These calibrated depth gauges were a reasonably accurate and foolproof method of weighing the boat's payload. Their origin goes back to old Archimedes himself. The water displacement of a boat equates directly to its weight. As its displacement can be measured on a scale calibrated to each boat, the weight of cargo on board can thus be calculated. Once the lock-keeper was happy in the knowledge that the entire dispatched load was still intact and that none had fallen off the back of a boat so to speak, he filled in the paperwork and the time bill. With the light work out of the way, the physical graft would begin. The casks were manhandled up unto the quay, for which the men received a few cents (of our money), per tonne. It was hard and back-breaking work, the like of which is unknown today. But while I am still a relatively young man, I recall unloading twenty-five tonne lorry loads of bagged fertiliser by hand, in fifty kg bags. I do not think for a minute that it is a particularly good comparison, but it nonetheless illustrates how many years were to pass before the bulk handling of goods was completely mechanised. It was the widespread adoption of the forklift truck and the ubiquitous wooden pallet that ultimately revolutionised materials handling.

By the year of 1969, after the passage of thirty years on the lock, Thomas Murphy Jnr was worn and weary and suffering from ill health. His sister Essie was married by this time, to John Conroy, who worked on the canal boats. Brother and sister and her husband and child all lived in the cottage but because of his occupation, Conroy was not there much of the time. Murphy was no longer able to carry out his work and so a successor was needed. If no one in the family could continue on as lock-keeper, they would all have to vacate the cottage forthwith. There was only one person from within the family that could realistically take the position. Conroy wished to remain on the boats, as the money was marginally better. Young Jimmy was not yet old enough. History was in danger of repeating itself. Thus the lot fell to Essie who thankfully was chomping at the bit to become the new lock-keeper. But there was a problem, about which she could seem to do very little. She was a woman. The Grand Canal Company (GCC) did not favour female lock-keepers.

There have been many formidable canal women over the years and Esther Conroy, despite being small in stature, is a very strong, articulate and resolute woman. No man in the Grand Canal Company would be a match for her. She would carry on the family tradition. She would be Lowtown's new lock-keeper. The fact that she was a woman had nothing whatsoever to do with it. The GCC were having none of it. It was beside the fact that there was already one female lock-keeper in their employment. They had no wish for another. It is important to remember that in 1969 the public service ban that prevented married women from holding their jobs in the civil service was still in operation. The GCC was part of the state public transport monolith, Coras Iompair Eireann. By extension, the odds were firmly stacked against Essie, given that her husband was not only alive and well, but also in work. But to steal a phrase from another tough woman from the last century, the lady was not for turning. Essie was installed as lock-keeper before 1969 was out. She continued in her post until 1983.

However life was to deal her another blow. In 1983 she suddenly became ill and was diagnosed with a brain tumour. Surgery was successfully carried out and Essie's brain was restored to being as sharp as ever. But it was time to hand over the baton to her son, Jimmy Conroy, who is now the present lock-keeper. However that old chestnut of a place to live was to surface again. The OPW (who were now responsible for the canals) had plans for a new lock-keeper's cottage for over twenty years. They were now, at long last, in a position to build it but conditionally required Essie to forsake her old cottage and move into the new house with her son and his family. She was not to be allowed to remain in the old family home. Thankfully good sense prevailed and Mrs Esther Conroy is still happily ensconced there twenty five years later.

9. A Million Miles Away

⚮

On a mild and dry Saturday morning in late April, I decided to take *The Tom Rolt* up the Milltown feeder. As I have previously mentioned this navigable channel joins the Old Barrow Line at Littletown, which is a couple of kilometres from Robertstown. This feeder channel draws its water from a number of springs in Pollardstown Fen and conveys it for a contorted 10km to supply the Grand Canal. As the Milltown feeder carries a navigation warning – due to a low bridge – restricting its use to boats with a draught of less than 0.75metre and a maximum height of 1.80 metre, my son wisely counselled that before we set off all gung-ho in the boat, we should check it out on foot first. As we were driving through Allenwood on our way down to the boat, he instructed me to take a right turn for Milltown.

'You'd be better to have a look at that feeder, before we head off up it in the boat,' son instructs me.

'Why?' I said, enthusing 'course we'll get up it, we don't need a lot of water and the bridge is hardly that low. It's not the QE2 you know.'

I could see the start of a slight father/son disagreement. It's not that either of us is argumentative, it's just that we wouldn't always agree and then we can't agree to disagree.

'I don't think for a minute that it is the QE2. It couldn't be further from it. The jacks would be bigger on the QE2 than your entire boat,' son retorts. Oh the joys of teenagers. But I would try again.

'Do you remember the day we got lost in the car up around Kilmeague and we saw the feeder and I said it looked alright to travel up?' I asked, with the slightest hint of reservation beginning to creep into my mind. Son wasn't having any of it.

'No you didn't,' he impatiently retorts, 'you said that the feeder was only fit for a wally in a canoe. Even Bertie Ahern has a better memory than you, Dad. If you lose any more memory cells you'll have none left.' Son had hit a raw nerve. There was little doubt and lots of evidence that my recall was not as good as it once was. But to admit this would be foolish.

'It's not that my memory is bad. It's just that when you reach my age there's an awful lot of information crammed in there and my retrieval systems are becoming overloaded,' I responded, adding 'will I turn right or not?'

'Yes,' son tells me, 'otherwise we will be up shit creek with nowhere to turn.'

Son was, of course, quite right. We drove up to Pluckerstown Bridge and it was low. Much too low. Not only that, the waterway is both narrow and shallow. To have gaily travelled down the feeder in the boat would have been a recipe for disaster with absolutely no place to turn. And it's not easy to reverse a narrow boat – even more difficult than it is the QE2. However it was disappointing that we wouldn't be able to take the boat down the channel. Sometimes you get all psyched up about something in particular and it's a very deflationary (and humiliating) process to have to climb down. However our despondency was not to last for long. This is a gorgeously secluded little waterway – the trees and bushes along the bank were a beautiful shade of a luxuriant green and the water was crystal clear to the bottom. Sufficiently tempted by what we had seen, we decided to explore it in its entirety between a combination of walking and driving (it's over 10km miles long).

We began at Huband Bridge, where the feeder deposits its clear water into the main body of the canal. As it's the summit level there are, intriguingly, three possible routes for this spring water. Some of this will flow in a south westerly direction – via the River Shannon and Limerick – eventually spilling into the wild Atlantic Ocean, which seems like a million miles away from central Kildare. And some will be liberated into St George's Channel – via the River Barrow and Waterford – while the rest of its water will flow – via the River Liffey – in an easterly direction to enter the Irish Sea at Ringsend. It never ceases to amaze me how all flowing water eventually finds its way to the sea.

As we traced the smooth path of twisting water back to its source in Pollardstown Fen, we came to its Achilles' heel, the aforementioned modern, low-level bridge at Pluckerstown. This is a basic concrete utilitarian structure – something like the Soviet Army in retreat might have hurriedly built – and typical of the type that respective county councils built across the canals in the 1960s and 70s. Then there was a very obvious attempt to destroy our canal heritage, what with low-level bridges, the de-watering of branch lines and the destruction of canal buildings, be they hotels or warehouses. And this vulgar activity would have been much more prevalent were it not for the good auspices of the IWAI and the Irish Georgian Society. These pioneering people cried 'stop' when everyone else understood progress to mean the total obliteration of everything that was built pre the foundation of the Irish Free State. At one stage in the early 1970s, matters reached a new low when a certain Fianna Fail Minister for Local Government actively sought the removal of Dublin's Georgian buildings, as an unwanted legacy of our colonial past. It was only the courageous voices of a few campaigners that halted this destructive lunacy. We owe these people an eternal debt.

The Milltown feeder continues to meander along the contours at the base of the Hill of Allen. This wooded hill, erupting suddenly as it does out of the flat Kildare plains, looked quite stunning in its late spring glory of new and fresh greens and transitional yellows. But this is, sadly, only a mask. The hill has fallen prey to the Celtic Tiger's enormous appetite for stone, sand and gravel. This outstanding hill is being devoured in a manner that is frightening. If the Roadstone Company has its way there will be precious little left of the Hill of Allen but the spoil heaps and pit waste, in a few short years. I have just criticised the authorities and others, in earlier years, for allowing the decimation of some of our canal heritage. But heritage destruction is, by no means, consigned to history. Big multinational interests have an insatiable greed to convert precious finite resources that are irreplaceable into fat director's salaries and handsome dividends to their shareholders. And sadly we cannot rely on Government to stop them in their tracks. As I write this the Meath countryside is threatened with another form of heritage abuse and emanating from a semi-state company. Eirgrid, the State controlled power transmission company intends to build a massive 400kV over ground power line marching across the north Leinster countryside. The day and age of such wanton abuse and disrespect for our rich heritage must surely be over, when there are feasible alternatives. But the hand of Government can be brutish and insensitive. While the voice of the people may be, all too often, ignored by the politicians, it is we – the people – who are the true guardians of the countryside.

Having cleansed my mind of these disturbing thoughts, it is refreshing to return to this peaceful little water. Just before the village of Milltown there lies a very quaint and narrow accommodation bridge which provides a lovely viewing platform to survey all around you.

There is a fine row of chestnut trees which must have surrounded a house of which nothing remains, while the majestic old mill building lies ruinous beside the water. We proceeded on to reach Milltown Bridge – which was the terminus for passenger boats in bygone days. It is now better known for its fascinatingly named (and much acclaimed) pub The *Hanged Man's*, apparently so called after the tragic end of a lovesick canalman in earlier times. Consistent with my thinking on the naming of boats, I find it interesting to see public houses or hotels called after a particular event (not necessarily a tragic one) or a person of note rather than the more mundane name of the proprietor. Once past the bridge, the countryside has changed with the good farmland becoming marginalised into a marshy, reed covered wetland which is, nonetheless, serenely beautiful.

In a previous chapter, I recounted how it was the engineer William Jessop who identified the multiple springs of Pollardstown Fen as the principal water source for the entire canal. It was thus with a great sense of history that we followed his now dividing channels – at the rather pretentiously named, Point of Gibraltar – deeper into the fen. As there were three of us and with no adults within earshot, other than my semi-adult and now reconciled son, I decided that we should now re-enact the inaugural visit of the three engineers. It seemed only right and proper to mark the occasion with a simple piece of theatre. Hence son was given the lead role of the senior English engineer, John Smeaton. I felt he would be better at his leading role than me as my memory could act up on some of the lines. To display obvious memory loss for the second time in a morning would be downright silly. I took the lesser role of William Jessop – and producer – and our youngest (age 7) played the understudy engineer, William Chapman. As Chapman's earlier career was as an agent for the steam engineers Boulton and Watt, which was, in fact, what brought him to Ireland in the first instance, he was probably a bit disillusioned with the whole idea. He presumably would have much preferred to sell the Grand Canal Company a colossal steam pump to lift water out of the Liffey and into the canal.

With the cast chosen and the lines given out, the stage was set for the curtain on this one act play.

Smeaton: [late fifties, top hatted, black riding boots, pointing his riding crop] 'I say, Jessop, old fellow, I can't [producer's note: pronounced 'kont'] see the point in driving this channel into this mire. It will destroy the bloody shooting, if nothing else. Good Lord, isn't there enough water in this barren and strife-torn land without coming up here? Ye ancient and wild Irishman will appear from the shadows and devour us all. I shan't go any further.'

Jessop: [(who looked quite like an eighteenth century Bertie Ahern, with whom I have no similarities whatsoever but that aside, I was more than happy to play the part) also top hatted, brown boots, pencil and scrolled up parchment in hand] 'Sir, please allow me to explain what I perceive to be the most intelligent and expedient method to execute a most excellent water source for this great canal. In yonder... .....'

Smeaton: [looking agitated, stroking his sideburns at the base of his jaw.] 'Jessop, cut the crap, just get on with it.' My son, clearly getting impatient, was already tired of the game and had deviated from the script.

Jessop: [slightly thrown by his boss's impatience] Sir, hither fen will – God willing – yield forth an abundant water supply from hence forth and into eternity. Moreover, I am occasioned to the belief that within this tumultuous wilderness there are greater in number than two score and five different springs, by the grace of God.'

[Producer's note, since Smeaton had become irritable I nodded to Chapman to enter]

Chapman: [bowler hatted, late twenties, clearly nervous in such elevated company] 'Mr Smeaton, Sir, Mr Jessop and I are opined that this wilderness will be drained to goodly effect and the water so extracted will … ….' ' [Producer's note, I was listening transfixed to my 7 year old daughter and thought she was well on her way to her first Oscar.]

'Dad?' the young Chapman says, 'I've forgotten what comes next?' Thank God for the innocence of small children. Teenagers are much more difficult. Poor Chapman never got an opportunity to put a plug in for Boulton and Watt. Smeaton was starting to march around in the squigy ground and was probably about to exit the scene.

'Cut.' I said, with all the authority of Quentin Tarantino, afraid of losing face.

We continued our walk through the fen following the reducing channel. At the end of one of the cuttings came the gurgling sound of gently flowing water. I knelt on the ground and pulled back the overhanging grass. Underneath where we stood was a small perfectly arched stone culvert, through which the water appeared. This was the source of one of the seminal springs, the sum of which fed and sustained the great body of water that is the Grand Canal. I reached down and touched the cut stones. Stones that William Jessop had ordered into place, two hundred and twenty five years ago. There were dogs barking in the far off distance. The touches of late spring were all around and the sedges and rushes moved gently on the fen. It was a scene that has changed little in all those years. My mind returned once more to those pioneering engineers and their labour force who toiled away in the absolute remoteness of this place, with a very clear vision of what they wanted to achieve. It was a surreal and memorable experience.

1. Picture of the author (in foreground) on what was clearly a bad hair day!

2. The 33rd Lock at Belmont, Grand Canal

3. Tullamore

4. The 26th Lock near Tullamore

5. *The Tom Rolt* at the old Kilbeggan Line, Ballycommon

6. New N6 road bridge crossing the dewatered Kilbeggan Line

7. Locke's Distillery, Kilbeggan

8. Lowtown 1957

(Shortall Collection, courtesy of Paddy Shortall)

9. The 19th Lock, Lowtown 1957
(Shortall Collection, courtesy of Paddy Shortall)

10. View from Fenton Bridge, Lowtown 2008

11. Levitstown Mill

12. Lifting Bridge at Levitstown

13. Maganey Bridge, River Barrow

14. Construction of Carlow sugar factory harbour 1926.
(Photo courtesy of Carlow County Museum)

15. Beet arriving at Carlow c.1926.
(Photo courtesy of Carlow County Museum and Irish Sugar Ltd.)

16. Sugar factory almost demolished 2007

17. All that remains of a once proud industry 2008

18. Gerry and the author Carlow 2007

19. The author at Milford Cut, River Barrow

20. Milford Weir

21. Milford Mill and Bridge, River Barrow

22. Grand Canal Dublin, 1957
(Shortall Collection, courtesy of Paddy Shortall)

23. Robertstown 1957
(Shortall Collection, courtesy of Paddy Shortall)

24. Robertstown 2007

25. Burgh Bridge, Main Line Grand Canal

26. Leinster Aqueduct, Main Line Grand Canal

27. Landenstown Lock, Main Line Grand Canal

28. Dredger boat, Royal Canal

29. Quaker Graveyard Rosenallis Co. Laois

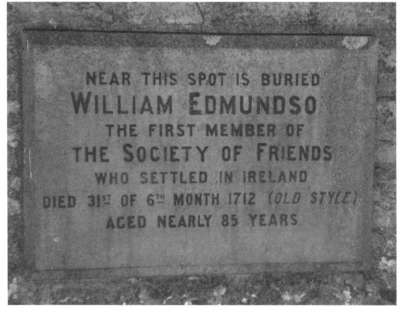

NEAR THIS SPOT IS BURIED
WILLIAM EDMUNDSO
THE FIRST MEMBER OF
THE SOCIETY OF FRIENDS
WHO SETTLED IN IRELAND
DIED 31ST OF 6TH MONTH 1712 (OLD STYLE)
AGED NEARLY 85 YEARS.

30. Quaker Graveyard Rosenallis Co. Laois

31. Departing Lowtown for the Shannon

32. The motley crew – Max, Holly and Alison

10. Smoke on the Water

⌘

It was now early summer and the weather was particularly good. It was high time to move on. I was keen to explore the River Barrow later on in the summer and decided that we should travel down in that direction. We set off from Lowtown on a Sunday morning, with no particular destination to reach by the end of the day. This is the preferred way for one to travel on the canal as there has to be an element of allowing time for events to unfold as you journey along. Deadlines for destinations have no place and would largely defeat the purpose of leisurely cruising along the water. But this relaxed and laid back approach to the use of one's time is an acquired discipline. For some this unfortunately may take a lifetime of frenzied rushing around to realise its utter futility while to others it comes naturally at birth. As for me, I arrived ahead of schedule into this world and it is a habit that has not improved with age. Equally – while the habits of a lifetime will die hard – I do hope that when it's nigh time for me to exit the stage, it's an appointment that I'll be late for.

We were all in our good spirits as we passed Ballyteague Castle, and my crew were competent enough to lock ourselves through. The canal, below Ballyteague, is once more traversing boggy low-lying land and is carried in a great, broad-shouldered embankment. We shortly came to the aqueduct crossing the River Slate. I can never resist the opportunity to stop the boat – provided time allows – as we cross an aqueduct and this one was no exception. It is not the finest example of the bridge builder's craft but it is, nonetheless, a substantial three arched structure.

I walked down the steep grassy bank to the river below. Remedial work had been carried out in mass concrete some years ago and while the work is sound, it does not exhibit the same craftsmanship as went into the original construction. Functionality and good craftsmanship may achieve the same requisite purpose but there is seldom beauty or pleasure in an item that is strictly functional. Somewhat predictably, my mind slips back to the construction of these beautiful stone structures. I think of all the different craftsmen's skills that were required to build such an aqueduct; from teams of navvies digging out foundations, while another labouring crew were hauling stone from a quarry onto the site. The stone cutters, perhaps with the luxury of a basic roof over their heads, laboured away meticulously cutting the stone with mallet and chisel to the exact replica of a wooden template made by a master craftsman. The stone masons busy at their work, assisted by apprentices physically hoisting up the cut stones and placing them on a bed of lime mortar, which was a mixture of hydraulic lime, sand and water. It was important that stone did not touch stone, as this could lead to structural cracking; a solid bed of mortar to spread the load between the stones was a very necessary requirement. Because the onset of frost would adversely affect the setting action of the mortar, the actual building of the stonework could only take place when the threat of frost was gone. And whether you accept global warming or not, the fact that the climate has changed is a certainty; the winters were a lot colder a couple of hundred years ago. In a severe winter it's likely that there was thick ice on still water for absolute weeks on end. The final course of stonework laid before the onset of winter was covered in straw and soil to protect the mortar from freezing. However excavations and stone carting and cutting could continue throughout the winter months.

Once the base walls were up a metre or so from the river, the arches began to extrude from the stone abutments. A wooden arched template, known as the falsework, was constructed by the carpenters. This was an elaborate timber affair made to the exact curve of the required stone arch and very strongly supported by props rising from the riverbed. As the wedge shaped stones – known as voussoirs – of the arch were laid on this wooden falsework, it was required to support a massive downward load until the stone arch became closed and thus self-supporting. When the keystone was cut and ceremoniously paced in position, the moment of truth had arrived. With not a little trepidation, the engineer would summon the carpenters and instruct them to drive out the wooden wedges that would loosen the wooden falsework. With the final blow of the sledge hammer the wedge would fly free of its load and the falsework would tumble down. If the stone arch, which it had supported, was properly built it remained standing free and proud. The stone masons would stand back in admiration and congratulate themselves on the beauty of their creation. Loaded carts could now use the aqueduct to cross the river, which would immediately facilitate the construction of the canal.

I clambered back up the embankment to the canal and judging by the faces of my crew, I had been studying the arches for a bit longer than I had realised.

'What were you at, Dad?' asks my son, who has obviously been appointed head of the tribunal of enquiry.

'Oh, I was just admiring the workmanship of the aqueduct,' I replied a bit flatly, disappointed that I should have to account for my (precious) time out. 'Well, see your man?' my son questions, pointing at a boat lying at anchor a few metres downstream, 'he's not very happy with you.' My eyes followed the pointing finger. My son's assessment appeared to be correct; the crew did not look too at ease with me. 'Oh, he'll be OK,' I reassured my son. We moved off the aqueduct and thus re-opened the canal to traffic after the temporary closure. As we passed the large cruiser, the skipper took a disparaging look at me and my boat and said;

'You'd be better to fit a jacks on that boat and not be holding everyone up.' There was little point in explaining the real reason for our delay on the aqueduct, so I decided it would be a pity to disappoint him.

'Jacks?' I said, 'what on a boat? I'd be better to put one in at home first.' My friend shook his head and powered up his large diesel motors, while his beautiful little children watched the Simpsons on colour TV. Different, different world, I thought. Everyone has their own reasons for cruising on the canal.

Once you depart the aqueduct it's a pleasant run along the embankment to Glenaree. We entered the lock and my son, who was in charge of operations ashore, closed the upper gates behind us. He then proceeded to wind up the racks in the lower gates and the boat started to descend. The journey was going along nicely and the morning was becoming lovely and sunny. I slipped off into a meditative other world – it was that sort of a day – and I became quite oblivious to what was going on around me. This is not a good idea if you are at the wheel of a car or locking a boat through.

I was deep in thought about the boat's engine. I had decided some weeks earlier to bite the bullet and pull out the unreliable and dirty and polluting engine. Not many people have to sleep with a diesel engine in their bedroom. Unfortunately that is exactly the situation on some narrow boats, not least of which is *The Tom Rolt*. The engine is boxed into a low compartment at the foot of the master's bed. Every little drop of diesel that leaked into the bilge during its working day will slowly and surely diffuse its unpleasant aroma throughout the cabin. The problem becomes more acute when you turn in to bed to rest your weary bones for the night. The tinge of diesel specifically targets the sleep activator part of your brain with horrendous consequences. Sleeping, as a result, becomes very elusive and well nigh impossible. You eventually slip off into the ultra lite version of slumber which graduates into a type of sleep.

However, your problems are not over yet. In fact, they're only beginning. The hint of diesel in the air permeates into the world of dreamland. Consequently all of your dreams revolve around oil. On one such awful dreamy occasion, I was on a massive oil tanker crossing the Gulf of Oman. On vessels of this size you need a small motorbike to get from one end of the ship to the other. My brother-in-law (another one) was a radio officer on such tankers and even though he was from a dairy farm and well used to chasing after cows, he was wasting too much time walking from one end of the ship to the other and they speeded him up with a motorbike. And true to reality, there was one provided for me and this part of my dream was very pleasant. I was whizzing up and down the tanker deck under the bluest of blue Arabian skies. I'd say I spent an hour on that motorbike (in real dream time) doing wheelies and power slides and you name it. But like a bold child, I got a bit too cocky. The front wheel of the bike collided with the raised corner of an opened hatch. I was catapulted down into the gigantic black hold, which was, at the very least, half full of the finest Arabian crude oil. The bike followed me on the way down and, being a bit heavier than I was, it started to overtake me. The hot exhaust pipe seared my leg as it passed, presumably seeking revenge for the bike's imminent fate. We both hit the crude oil with an almighty splash and I tried courageously to swim. But even at the best of times, I couldn't swim a stroke to save my life and I had no hope whatsoever in the thick, sticky crude oil. The bike disappeared down into the blackness with a loathsome gurgling noise. The oil went up my nose and out through my ears. I hadn't a snowballs chance in hell of survival. The proverbial tunnel of light that people who have almost died tell us about was beginning to take shape. I was definitely on the way out and was as close to death as I've been in a good few years. However, there was little clue, as I began to die, as to which way I was going, whether up to my eternal reward or down for a hot and heavy interview with Old Nick. Nor did I feel the great sense of peace and of deep overwhelming love that some people talk about.

Some time ago, I remember reading that the Australian media tycoon, Kerry Packer, suffered a near death experience. His heart was actually stopped, for a few moments, and so he was clinically dead. But he recovered and when asked by a journalist what it was like to be dead, he replied 'believe me, Son, there's nothing out there.' He has died properly since.

Now, I accept that my near death experience wasn't quite as real as Packer's was because, on the contrary, my heart was actually going like the clappers. However, I would still like to take a more optimistic viewpoint about the hereafter. I'd say there is something out there. But any more than that, I can't tell you. Anyhow my time on earth was not yet up and I awoke in a trembling, oily sweat. It took a little while for me to realise that I wasn't actually dead but that I was, in fact, mad alive. However this had been a particularly nasty oily dream and in fairness, not all the smelly diesel engine induced dreams had such unpleasant ends.

On another oily dream night I was back in the 1980s and at the Oil Baron's Ball in Dallas, Texas, the annual one J. R. Ewing used to go to. And that was one mighty night. I got on famously with Crystal Carrington, remember her (the tall, willowy, fifty something blonde with the shoulder pads)? I won't go into the details here but suffice to say I thought it was an awful pity that I woke up at all.

However in reality and on balance, there were far more negatives to this diesel tainted cabin than there are positives. If the smelly and leaky diesel engine was fitted outside of the cabin and underneath the deck, it would obviously be much less of an issue, as it is on a cruiser-style narrow boat. But there is yet another problem that would not be solved by such a relocation. On all narrow boats you stand on the deck right over the outlet of the exhaust pipe as you steer the boat along. There isn't another machine on the planet which has the same lethal arrangement. The fumes rise up along your left trouser leg and start to mushroom out at around shoulder height. Your head ends up enveloped in a toxic ball of death containing carbon dioxide, nitrous oxide, sulphur dioxide and every other known and unknown greenhouse gas. Whether these fumes are entirely to blame for global warming, climate change, melting of the polar ice caps, the rise in sea levels and even wetter Irish summers, I am not entirely convinced. But I am convinced that they don't do me personally any good. Neither are my old lungs the finest bit of my anatomy – they never have been through no fault of my own. I can't breathe with these fumes all around and I fall into a fit of coughing that could well have terminal consequences. And health issues aside, I smell like a right grease monkey. Consequently, all of this exposure to diesel fumes has made me very aware of hydrocarbon pollution. I am by no means what you would call a green, alternative type, in fact, I am far from it. I don't buy into the elitist organic food fallacy or wear sandals nor do I have a ponytail. I don't harp on and on about composting and hybrid cars and insulation. Our house is a shameful temple to thermodynamic inefficiency and has more heat loss and drafts than a cave. But I am conscious of the beauty of the world around me and of the fragility of life in all its different forms. I have no wish to damage the environment, in so far as it is possible. Standing on the stern of *The Tom Rolt* has made me aware of the awfulness of the emissions from old, worn and outdated diesel engines.

There could be no doubt about it. The engine must go. Life is too short to be spoiled by such afflictions. I did not need to share my life with such an objectionable object. I had no loyalty to this repugnant product of the Ford Motor Corporation. But I had nothing against Ford *per se*. In fact, it was quite the opposite. I knew that Henry Ford was of Irish extraction and that he was a brilliant engineer and he went on to make some fine tractors and cars. So much so, I have always promised myself that some day, when the kids are at least half educated and look like somebody might ultimately employ them, I would splash out on a 1920s Cork built Fordson Model N tractor to add to my small vintage collection. I was also aware of the fact that Henry (the first) invented the assembly line and that he got this very idea from watching the Chicago meat plants in the methods they used to disassemble the steers for meat, and everything else, as they progressed down through the factory. No, there was little doubt, Henry was an alright decent fellow. I had nothing against him.

So how did his ancestors end up making such a desperate engine, and him such a smart fellow? I don't know the answer. But probably what happened was the same as with many another family. They got too big for their boots and didn't want to do a whole lot themselves, except maybe shoot wild boar in Pennsylvania and grouse in Connemara. They employed a load of nit-wits to run the company. And then fifty years or so later, they employed a particular twit who couldn't design an eggcup and told him to design a new diesel car engine. I had the misfortune to buy a boat engined with the results of his handiwork. Not that there was anything wrong with the rest of the boat, its fine. She's just like a very fit tennis player with a beautiful body who has developed a dodgy heart. With a transplant she's be… …..

'Hey Dad,' my son shouted, from his commanding position on the planks of the deep lock gate. Unsure of whether he had a communication line open to me, he tried again, much louder;

'Dad, Earth to Dad, quick, the boats gone all slopey. You're not watching it, you're daydreaming.'

He was right. Horror of absolute horrors, the stern of the boat had come down on the sill of the upper gates. I had stopped the boat too close to the gates and as the lock emptied, the rudder and the skeg – which is the lower rudder support and is fixed just under the propeller – came down firmly on the protruding stone sill (which is like a big stone step). Meanwhile, as the lock continued to empty, the bow was still floating in the descending water and the boat was beginning to take a drastic downhill look.

Hindsight is a wonderful thing. It is all too easy to be wise after the event. Post mortems invariably highlight the obvious errors which lead to an accident. I very quickly realised what was happening. But I was extremely naïve in that I had allowed the incident to happen, as it was common sense. There was absolutely no doubt that I was not paying due attention. I had been in another world altogether. I was guilty as sin.

The wisest thing to do in such a situation is to immediately shut down the racks, thus containing what water that remains in the chamber. A lock-keeper would almost certainly have done this and at lightning speed. But with all due respect to my son, he would not have known to do this and neither would he have been quick enough to act. Had I taken the time to shout this instruction up to him and for him to carry it out, it would have been too late. The stern would have remained perched on the sill while the bow fell with the decreasing water level. The boat would then have, more than likely, flipped over in the lock and the consequences could be very serious.

There was only one other possible option to try and prevent disaster. It carried a high degree of risk of causing damage to the boat. But it was Hobson's choice. There was nothing for it. I quickly shoved the propulsion lever forward, hoping that there was still enough water around the propeller to allow it to push the boat forward and hence off the sill. I was lucky, very lucky. The boat slid forward with a grating noise and eased herself of the sloping sill. She was free and back in the water.

Disaster had been avoided, but the tiller handle didn't feel hectic. There was still a reasonable degree of steering – and certainly good enough to get us out of the lock and to moor at the jetty – but the tiller was as sloppy as a spoon in a cup of tea. I was afraid that the damage could be pretty severe and would warrant towing the boat back up to Lowtown for a lift out of the water. That would have been so humiliating. The whole world would be able to see what I had done. Please, please, God, don't let it be. I couldn't bear that my pride would be so mortally wounded. Some of the lowest points in life are after an accident, usually in the car. Yes, of course, you are extremely relieved that no one is hurt – and that you're still alive – but you just feel so unlucky, so annoyed with yourself – and with everyone else – so humiliated and so alone. And the rest of the World is very happy to stand and stare at the damage you have done. You just want to melt and disappear.

Being of a mechanical mind it was quickly obvious what was wrong. The weight of the descending boat had been borne by the rudder on the stone sill. Very fortunately, the skeg had remained clear of the sill and so was unaffected, as was the propeller. The rudder was pushed up out of its lower socket and then it proceeded to smash the top bearing. It was all fixable with the boat in the water and right where it was, and no one would be any the wiser.

While we are all capable of making stupid mistakes from time to time, this was a particularly stupid one. There is precious little that I can offer in my defence but there are two relevant points that I wish to make, in the vain hope that it will allow me a very small degree of credibility. Firstly, no one warned me about this potential danger. I had to learn the hard way. Keep as far away from the sill as possible, when locking down. Some sills are dangerously long; Glenaree, Lock

No.22B is a case in point. You may think that you are clear of the sill but it may still be lurking under your stern. Secondly, locking a boat up or down is a potentially dangerous exercise. There are many things that can go wrong. Vigilance is required by both the crew of the boat and the acting lock-keeper. Until you are well versed on the procedure, it's very wise to seek experienced help.

A few weeks after this mishap, I saw a sobering picture in the British canal newspaper, *Towpath Talk*. It depicted a narrow boat on its side in the bottom of a lock. It too had been 'silled' on a lock. Thankfully the crew were unhurt. It was righted by a crane, pumped out and then refloated. I could have starred in the *Inland Waterway News*.

11. Times Past and Present

◦◦◦

In the interval that *The Tom Rolt* lay at Glenaree, for repairs to the rudder, the replacement engine had arrived in from England. I had ordered a new, Japanese built, Kubota diesel engine which was marinised by an English company, Beta Marine, who specialise in boat engines. For those of you who are unfamiliar with this terminology, I will briefly explain. To marinise an engine is to eliminate the conventional cooling fan and radiator and set the engine up whereby it uses canal/river water as a coolant either directly or indirectly. There are other modifications as well but there's little need to bother you with these.

Coincidentally, there is a connection between the company, Beta Marine and L. T. C. (Tom) Rolt. This company was formed by some former staff of the well known engine manufacturer R. A. Lister & Co. Listers were founded in 1867 and developed a worldwide reputation for their diesel engines, water pumps and agricultural machines. There are a great many canal boats still powered today with the ubiquitous Lister SR3 diesel engine. In 1986 Listers merged with an old rival to form Lister-Petter Ltd, a very large manufacturing concern with a global presence. But in an earlier age, the young Rolt finished out his apprenticeship with the Lister brothers. He spent a happy and formative year or two there, largely in machine design, shortly after the development of their first diesel engine in 1929. While I have been familiar with Lister engines for many years, it was another of their machines that I knew more intimately and ultimately came to despise.

As a child and into my early teens, a small flock of sheep were kept on the farm. They were the responsibility of the herdsman, known simply and affectionately to us all by his surname, Carr. He had lived and worked on the farm since Adam was a boy and while he was a very decent sort he could, like most of us, become a little hot under the collar from time to time. Every year as the weather started to warm up, the sheep would have to be shorn. Carr disliked this task and would put it off for as long as possible, citing all sorts of excuses some plausible, others less so. However my father would claim that he saw a ewe in the advanced stages of heat induced exhaustion and Carr would be instructed to stop procrastinating and get on with the job. Unlike today, wool was then a valuable commodity; now its value doesn't cover the cost of shearing. There was a Lister shearing machine for this purpose – it was very ancient and probably dated from Rolt's Lister days. The paint had long since faded away, so much so that there was little clue as to its original colour. Carr would appear of a warm morning in late April with the flock of sheep following behind him. His faithful collie dog – Jessie IV – would form the rearguard to keep the reluctant and wise old stragglers in check. The sheep were marshalled into a holding pen all the time nervously grinding their teeth while awaiting the onslaught that would deprive them of their woolly coats. My brother and I knew that Carr would come looking for us, within a very short time, to help with the work. We were an essential part of the process.

Our Lister shearing machine was not powered by electricity or engine or tractor. It used the oldest and most basic form of power known to man – his own physical effort. This human power source was also the most inconsistent in delivering steady, reliable motive effort. The machine was duly set up and a volunteer was required to turn a big wooden handle, which then powered the shears through a flexible drive cable. Two shearing heads could be operated off a single machine.

'Gerryeen,' (Carr added een to most people's names, hence Tomeen, Mickeen, Dickeen etc), 'start turnin' the handle.' The first woolly victim had been turned up on its back on the newly swept floor and everything was ready and waiting. Taking a deep breath I would reach up with my skinny arms and pull down the handle hoping that the downhill momentum would be enough to get the old Lister spinning properly.

'The curse o'jaysus on you, *garsún*, [a young lad] will you put your back into it?' As soon as Carr had buried the shears into the fleece it had caused a momentary power surge that was enough to stop the handle's rotation dead in about four nano-seconds. Undaunted, I heroically cranked her up again. Carr attacked the thick greasy fleece with gusto. The load peaked again and the handle visibly slowed but I managed to keep the wheel turning. All was going along fine, until the nerves got the better of the poor ewe and she piddled in a rainbow-like arc all over Carr's chest.

'The curse o' jaysus on you – you auld hoor.' Carr berated the ewe – it was beside the fact that the poor female sheep was retained on the farm for actually being promiscuous and a virtuous ewe would be of little use to mankind. I knew that I'd better try to keep the flywheel spinning and the power up. Within a few minutes the first lady looked as skinny and as roughly shaven – with a few bloody nicks – as a 1940s urchin following his mother out of the barber's shop.

I could take a well earned minute's rest while the fleece was carefully rolled up and thrown into the woolsack. Carr, who like most people, hated anyone to be idle while he was working, instructed us to clean off our boots and climb into the big sack and pack down the fleeces. Loose straw stuck to the fleece like Velcro and no self respecting shearer would tolerate a single straw in the woolsack. The next woolly creature was then caught and rolled over unto her back.

'Right *garsún*, away you go, there's another ninety of these feckers to be done,' Carr said. He picked up the second shearing head and gruffly offered it to Malone, who was the wool packer and general assistant, 'Malone, grab that auld hoor there and get going with this.'

Aughanish Alumina is, I think, the biggest electricity consumer in the country. When they start the massive motors there, the ESB down in Moneypoint power station know all about it. The normally smooth running giant turbines grunt and shiver in protest while the digital readouts on the voltmeters go into freefall. The start up of all the electrical gear in the aluminium plant has to be phased, in order to ease the load in gradually otherwise all of Limerick will be blacked out. The same technique should be applied to the gradual loading of the shearing machine but my shearing friends clearly knew nothing at all about this. The two shearers eagerly attacked the two sheep with the split second timing of two dancing partners in Riverdance. I completed the first revolution, thinking I might just be able for them – I would show them what I was made of.

Oh for the very foolish and naïve optimism of youth. I accelerated the handle on the downward arc but the uphill stroke was to be terminal. It was like Cassius Clay hit me a killer upper cut on the left eye, in round two. The handle stalled so suddenly that I was catapulted up and over the supporting stand and ended up in a humiliated heap in the woolsack.

'Right,' said Carr, 'where's Tomeen?' Tom(een) is my older brother.

The Lister shearing machine was never upgraded. Rather than go for one of their newer models, my father thought it better to get rid of the sheep altogether. It was a parental decision that my brother and I were very happy about. I think Carr was as well.

The jetty at Glenaree lock seemed to be as good a place as any to fit the new (Lister pedigree) engine. It was very unlikely that *The Tom Rolt* would be any closer to home in the near future. Anyhow, no matter what place that you could pick on the Grand Canal it all seems to be in or around an hour's boggy drive from my house. I rang up the fellow who I normally engage for this type of work and explained what was involved. Tony is an excellent mechanic and has a very droll sense of humour.

'Howya Tony, how's life, are you busy?' I asked. Tony might have to be humoured along.

'Ah, Ger Potterton, good morning to you.' It was just after six in the evening, as I had heard the Angelus on the radio.

'Tony, I have the new engine for the boat now. When would suit you to stick it in with me?' I made it sound very simple, like just an evening's work. This was a foolish mistake.

'Can you bring it up to me, Ger?'

'What, Tony?'

'The boat, can you bring the boat up to me, Ger?' Tony replies in a dead pan voice. I never know when he's being serious. Tony knew well what size the boat was. He had done the earlier service. I would try calling his bluff.

'What like, this evening, Tony?'

'Yeah, wait for an hour or two, Ger.' My ploy hadn't worked and while Tony had won the round, I felt the matter wasn't being properly addressed.

'Anthony, of course I can't bring it up to you, we'll have to bring the engine to the boat and fit it down in Rathangan,' I replied, trying to conceal the irritation in my voice.

'Where's Rathangan?' Tony asks, all innocently and then pipes up, before I had time to spell it out to him, 'Tell you what, Ger?'

'What, Tony?' I was becoming more exasperated by the minute.

'Bring it up to Ferran's Lock, tomorrow, and we'll do it there.'

Ferran's Lock is on the Royal Canal. To bring the boat from where she was lying to Ferran's lock would mean travelling back down the Grand Canal, up the Shannon and await for the re-opening to the Royal, sometime next year, and then finally down to Ferran's, which was close to Tony's place. Tony is quite familiar with the inland waterways system and would know that this wasn't realistic. I would have to be patient and bite my lip.

'Tony, you know as well as I do that is not a brilliant idea,' I firmly replied.

A date for the heart transplant on the boat was eventually agreed upon. But in common with the Health Service there was a waiting list to be worked through first. The acutely ill were at the top of the list and apparently my engine was not in this category. But I was patient, as Tony is the Maurice Nelligan of mechanics; he's good and well worth the wait. But we had another problem to surmount; how would we lift the engines in and out and all down on the bank of the canal? They are both heavy and awkward and particularly so in a confined space. I didn't really relish the idea of bouncing all the way from home to Glenaree with the JCB to do the honours. Tony had access to a mini digger so we agreed that it was a much better idea.

Early one May morning we set off with the replacement engine, a jeep full of tools and the digger in tow. Tony was in a stupor for coffee before he was inclined to do anything so we briefly stopped in Rathangan and that was sufficient to get him fired up. And so, suitably refreshed, we arrived at the boat and started work.

Within a few hours of steady activity we had the old Ford unit hanging on a sling from the digger.

'Ger, what do you want me to do with this?' asks Tony from the digger seat.

'Fire it into the canal, Tony, and good riddance to it,' I replied with a straight face, half serious.

Without a word, he revs up the digger, lifts up the jib and proceeds to swing the old filthy blue lump towards the centre of the canal.

'Tony,' I roared, 'I'm only messing.' While it would have been a fitting end, it was not the right thing to do and I had visions of the EPA arresting me for environmental pollution.

'Janey, Ger, I thought you were serious.' Anthony is a master of brinkmanship.

In keeping with the best traditions of TV cookery programmes, I had prepared most of the required engine adapter steel plates earlier. I was then able to whip them out, just at the right time, which greatly impressed the master chef. By late evening on that first day we were on target with the work. Yes, there were glitches and plenty of cursing (I was the principal offender in this regard as matters have to be very serious before Tony succumbs to profanities), when we bumped our heads on sharp corners that shouldn't be there or cut bits off fingers. But quite apart from the fact that we very nearly set the engine bay alight with the sparks from the grinder; we were winning. We set off for home, pleased with our progress and with a list as long as your arm of things we had forgotten to bring but were necessary to complete the installation.

It was several days later before time allowed us to return and finish the work. After a few fraught hours, as the tension was starting to build, we were ready to start the sea trials. With the slightest twist of the key, the Kubota fired up, and we pulled out into the canal.

'Love them or hate them but it's hard to beat the Japs.' So opined Tony as we headed off down towards Rathangan, using all three senses of sight, sound and smell to ensure everything was running as it should be. I was delighted with the way *The Tom Rolt* responded to her new heart and I think that old Tom himself would have been pleased with our efforts.

12. Mecca in Monasterevin

❧

O n a showery afternoon at the end of May, we departed Glenaree
with our sights set on Vicarstown, a not inconsiderable distance of 27km downstream. To travel this far in a car is just a half an
hour's run but in a leisurely canal boat this is long distance stuff and
could take days if not weeks depending on circumstances. It was a
pleasant run into Rathangan – which is the first town that you meet
– but the clouds were gathering into a great dark menacing mass that
filled the sky overhead. Within a matter of minutes the point of satu-
ration would occur and trigger the release of stair rods of water unto
the mortals below. As we passed under the new footbridge – which
fulfils its role in a very utilitarian manner – a boat entered the double
lock up ahead. We moored at the jetty just as the heavens opened,
allowing little time to batten down the hatches.

The people on the boat ahead were bound for Graiguenamanagh
(which we considered to be light years away) hoping to be there in
three days time. I felt this was extremely ambitious, not least because
of the weather. But the husband and wife crew were well equipped

with rain gear and had an earnest look of determination that suggested it would take more than a wet evening to let their schedule slip. The lock-keeper appeared as they left the lower chamber and we cast off our lines and swiftly locked through.

The old harbour in Rathangan is home to Canalways Ireland – who rent out boats – and there is usually an interesting collection of craft moored along the stone quay. One of these rental boats is a wide beam barge, painted in a similar blue and red colour scheme to our own. The similarity does not end there. The barge is also clearly named in commemorative fashion; it bears the legend *The James Gill* on its side. I was curious about this choice of name and in a later conversation with the boat's owner I learned that James Gill was the skipper of one of the last trading boats on the Grand Canal. The Gill family had a long connection with the inland waterways and I am delighted that this association still lives on. It also proved to me the validity of naming a vessel after a notable person of the waterways, rather than immortalising an unworthy teenage sweetheart or resorting to some silly cliché.

It is also pleasing to see that the Rathangan boats are well painted up and in bright colours. I feel that it is the use of bold, rich colours that set canal craft apart from the cruiser fraternity. Traditionally English narrow boat operators were very uninhibited in their generous use of bright colours. A considerable amount of money was spent on the paintwork, typically with coach lines, accurately painted and framing the cabin edges. The artwork on the English narrow boats was greatly influenced by that of the circus and the fairground. This is not surprising; the boat people also led a wandering, gypsy lifestyle that brought them from town to town. Many of these boats had bright geometric designs and symbols, with castles and roses being particularly popular. The owner's name was often meticulously emblazoned on the cabin side in shadowed letters with perhaps roses entwined around the capitals. Such a tasteful exhibition of the sign writer's craft must have been a particularly English thing, as you will still see examples of imaginative coach lines, scrolls and attractive lettering on the cab doors of modern day British trucks. However it is unlikely today that it is the work of a talented sign writer but more usually a computer generated graphic that is simply stuck on. Nonetheless, it still creates a very distinctive and traditional effect. In Ireland we do not seem, historically, to have ever taken the same pride in transport ownership, whether steam engine, canal boat or lorry. And certainly our canal trading boats were a case in point. These tended to be very drab in appearance, with paintwork more reminiscent of naval camouflage than anything else. The fact that the majority of these boats were owned by the Grand Canal Company may account for this but equally most of the English narrow boats were part of large company fleets. The Anderton Canal Carrying Company had up to 175 narrow boats in operation serving the pottery industry in Stoke-on-Trent. The tiller on the English narrow boat was the *pièce de résistance*. In a style typical of a fairground ride, two or three colours are braided around the metal tube of the tiller shaft. And to crown it all, the artwork adorning a simple metal watering can would be magnificent as the boat operators were prepared to pay an inordinate sum of hard earned money to have something beautifully unique.

With some very notable exceptions that I can think of, many of our present day canal craft wear a rather dreary and funereal coat. Neither do I include *The Tom Rolt* on the list of exceptions; it's somewhere in between. And the choice of colour can be an evocative thing to some people. When my wife saw *The Tom Rolt* for the first time it provoked an interesting remark;

'It looks really nice', she said, 'but you can't leave it in those colours.'

'Why? I think it looks great,' I said, adding, 'I always liked red and blue.'

'And white,' my wife replied.

'So?' I retorted feeling a little rebuffed. The white didn't count as it's not a real colour and it's only on the roof.

'You're like a floating Union Jack. People will think it's a Royal boat that belongs to the Queen or a very loyal citizen of the United Kingdom.' My wife was brought up in Northern Ireland and they were a very colour sensitive lot up there, at that time. Thankfully, that period of Irish history has now greatly moved on. And in the interests of unity – certainly within the marital unit – I should add that my wife and her family have always taken a very neutral stance.

'Trust you to notice – it never occurred to me – would you prefer if it were green white and orange?' I responded, a little unkindly.

'Green and yellow would be nice', she replied in her soft west Ulster accent, adding, 'leave out the white.'

It spilled rain with a vengeance for most of the way down to Macartney lock, where we caught up with our friends from Rathangan. This double lock is in an attractive setting but in the gloom of the wet evening its beauty was well diluted. The lock-keeper, who is also the bridge-keeper in Monasterevin, enquired of us as to whether we would need a bridge lift that evening. I told him that I really didn't know and that the only certainty was that we would pull in somewhere close to habitation very, very soon. We were all as wet as water rats and in dire need of food. My teenage crew were on the point of mutiny and communication with them had become very difficult. How that great Athy man, Ernest Shackleton, kept his crew from killing each other while stuck in the Antarctic ice, I shall never know. Could it ever be that a good soaking on a narrow boat in the Irish midlands, all of an April evening is actually more demoralising? I shall leave you to ponder that conundrum but if you have never experienced either you are happily disadvantaged. Our keeper, sensing our great need of landfall, advised us to moor in the harbour where there was a vacant berth.

As we rounded the corner, our travelling companions were tied up waiting for the bridge to be lifted. Rather than moor in the harbour, I thought it better to pass under the bridge while it was raised and then lie up on the other side. That way we wouldn't need to annoy the bridge-keeper on the Sunday morning. It is of course possible to pass through a lock single-handedly but a bridge-keeper is generally indispensable. I tried to convey my reasoning to the two teenagers but they were having none of it.

'Hello,' I shouted up to the wet huddled creatures in the bow of the boat preparing to throw a line ashore, 'I think we'll follow your man under the bridge, while it's up.'

'No, we won't.' The response was in absolute unison.

'Why not?' I enquired.

'Cos, then you'll keep going `till we're in Vicarstown,' came the reply from the hooded heads without so much as looking up.

'Don't be ridiculous, Vicarstown is absolute miles away,' I responded, somewhat indignantly.

'We know. That's exactly the point.'

'I promise I'll pull in after the bridge and before the next lock' – which was only around the corner – 'and I'm just as wet, probably even wetter, than you are.'

'Promise?'

'Promise,' I replied.

By the time this deal was closed the other boat was almost clear of the bridge and about to enter the aqueduct over the River Barrow. The bridge-keeper shouted across to us;

'Did you make your mind up yet? What are yis doing?'

'We're going to follow that boat,' I told him.

'Get a move on then, the traffic is backing up to Rathangan,' the bridge-keeper instructed us, the water running down his nose and dropping into the canal.

For those of you who are unfamiliar with this interesting old bridge, it is similar, in effect, to a railway level crossing. The public road is at the same level as the canal, which it traverses with this simple lifting steel platform. In earlier days, the bridge had to be winched up manually. The winding mechanism was electrified some years ago, which doesn't do much to speed the process up but it does require less physical effort. The whole procedure takes a short while and the traffic quickly builds up. I worry about what it tells you about my nature but I delight in crossing under this bridge and bringing the town to a standstill. It's an experience that shouldn't be rushed. And as far as I am concerned the more traffic that I hold up, the better. I relish the fact that I am travelling on an ancient mode of transport, which is oblivious to time and deadlines. Meanwhile, all these stressed out motorists fail to understand why their journey should be interrupted for a fool on a boat to dawdle across their road. I pause half-way over to see how long the queue is becoming, on either side. If it's not yet beyond the railway bridge, I could safely put in a little more time. It'd really make my day if there was a big black ministerial Mercedes stuck in the waiting traffic – I'd stop the boat there and then and feign a breakdown and have a picnic on the bank. It would be an awful shame to cross here early on a Sunday morning and miss all this excitement and annoy nobody. But like most things in life, you could overdo it. Once there is a cacophony of horns blowing, it's better to move on.

Once across the road, there's another treat in store. Monasterevin is Mecca for those who are into industrial archaeology, not least for its range of interesting bridges. The Grand Canal makes its one and only crossing of the River Barrow here in a splendid aqueduct which was completed by 1831. It is an elaborate combination of a wrought iron railing over three great stone arches. In 1785 the canal engineers had planned to enter the Barrow at this point and continue the navigation down the river to Athy. But this was found not to be practical due to low summer water levels as the river was close to its source and so it was decided to continue the excavation to Athy. But prior to the aqueduct's construction, the river was traversed by locking up and down either side which was a laborious process. From this elevated vantage point, one is blessed with a beautiful vista whichever way you care to look. In the westerly, downstream direction, you are treated to your first view of the descending river. There is undoubtedly something very magical about the River Barrow and I was immediately filled with rapturous desire to explore her mysteries in the summer weeks that lay ahead. Looking upstream, the Great Southern and Western Railway crosses the river in a majestic lattice girder bridge. In the open space between this and the aqueduct, the Community Council have created the attractive Riverside Park, which is a worthwhile amenity asset to the town. Such a creation helps the recent influx of new inhabitants to appreciate the indigenous beauty of what's on their doorstep. There is also a well maintained walk across the aqueduct, which we would explore later. The long-time closed Mountmellick Branch line – which was constructed in the 1820s – enters the main body of the canal here as it sweeps sharply left for the lock.

It was clearly not a case of 'miles to go before I sleep' but I did have a promise to keep and we happily pulled in to the jetty above the 25th lock. We would overnight here and it appeared to be a secluded area albeit in very close proximity to the town. Our first requirement was dry clothes followed by sustenance. We walked back across the aqueduct and up to the harbour. The rain had relented by now and the sun was breaking through with a shameless grin that was intended to evaporate all our memories of the torrential afternoon. As it was still early evening, there was plenty of time for the walking tour before nightfall. The harbour quarter in Monasterevin has been recently redeveloped with the building of what are architecturally pleasing apartment blocks. Some of the original harbour has been filled in – as has a short branch line into the centre of the town – but what remains of the harbour has been well integrated into what I think is an imaginative development. It is also very convenient to the train station, which from an environmental point of view constitutes a very sustainable commute for its inhabitants to the city. Leaving these new homes behind you, it is a pleasant walk up the old streets of the town. There is an unmistakable feeling of old grandeur about these streets, with Georgian houses strongly suggesting Monasterevin was a prosperous canal town with a merchant class not unlike Tullamore. And this was indeed the case; in the glory days of the canal there was a brewery, a distillery and a tobacco factory here. In that sense, as with many of these canal towns, all of the addictive pleasures of this life were well catered for. The more mundane food requirements of the local community and further afield were met by Ballykelly Mill which we had passed by on the canal bank coming into the town.

In the same manner as Tullamore is associated with the Charleville Estate, Monasterevin has its own very grand country house and demesne in Moore Abbey. Perhaps most notable as the former home of the world famous tenor, Count John Mc Cormack, this very significant early Georgian pile is now occupied by the Sisters of Charity of Jesus and Mary. Quite a few religious orders acquired old stately homes such as Moore Abbey, when they became unmanageable as private houses in the tumultuous period after the First World War. There are many examples of such around the country amongst which are Emo Court, Dunboyne Castle and Donamon Castle. While these religious orders may not, in every case, have been entirely sympathetic to the preservation of these heritage buildings, we should nonetheless be grateful for their intervention. Without these historically important buildings being put to a practical use such as seminaries, convents and schools, they may well have been demolished.

It is with a degree of guilt that I tell you that our dining that night was at the lower end of the market. I fear I may be creating the impression that our diet on the boat consists chiefly of fried and fast food. I am also aware that obesity has become a national issue and I would in no way want to be charged with perpetuating the problem. Not only that, I must confess to becoming a little annoyed whenever I see hugely obese people rapidly increasing their calorific intake with ever more chips and Coke. Moderation and discipline is good in all things. I can offer little in my defence of fried food except to say that; fortunately, neither my crew nor I are (yet) threatened with even the mildest form of obesity. Secondly we do eat lots of healthy stuff, like salad rolls and fruit – which I shall make a conscious effort to tell you more about – and we aspire to live on a staple diet of lentils and water the rest of the time. Within our walking range the choice was a toss-up between a pizza parlour or good old burger and chips. The chip shop was run by an Italian family; the people of that country are particularly good at making fast cars and fast food. We therefore ordered their finest cod and chips, which didn't disappoint. After a little shopping for the (healthy) bare essentials and an energetic calorie destroying walk we returned to *The Tom Rolt*.

Fellow narrow boat people had moored below the lock in our absence. It is always good to have company nearby when lying up for the night. Weather permitting; I like to sleep with the stern doors open. I have this (harmless) fantasy about sleeping with loads of fresh air but I am not brave enough to sleep entirely *al fresco*. Something might attack me like a rat or a bat or some such hairy nocturnal creature. While I would hate to have had tuberculosis, as was prevalent in bygone years, I do envy the way they slept on open verandas in the sanatoriums, all year around. It would be very safe as it were, up off the ground and with companions close by. Though, it must have been mighty difficult to get out of bed of a winter's morning. At home, I am forbidden by my wife to open our bedroom window fully except for the months of July and August. I could, of course, choose to sleep in another room, but that would have its disadvantages. I think it's preferable to be hot and stuffy, rather than cold and unloved.

I sleep lightly on the boat and awoke with a start at 5.30am. There was a terrible commotion going on and somewhere awfully close to the boat. The shouting and screaming was enough to suggest that someone was being physically attacked. With no wish to be next on the list, I jumped out of the nesting box, slammed the doors shut and barricaded up the inside with toolboxes and overalls and fold up chairs. I then retreated and curled up into a defensive position under the sheets. The danger passed over and we enquired next morning as to what was going on. Thankfully no one was killed – or even hurt – as it was only a few gurriers, well tanked up on their way home. It's probably just that I am not used to regular urban life. It's also fortunate that I wasn't sleeping *al fresco*.

13. Weir Worries

֍

We awoke to a mist lying on the water which was quickly dispersed by a jubilant sun beaming from a cloudless sky. The weather woes of yesterday evening would soon be forgotten. After a contrite whole grain cereal and juice breakfast we were quickly through the lock and around the very acute bend in the canal. It was a case of once bitten, twice shy. On a previous occasion, many years ago, this bend caught me unawares and I ended up with the boat's bow stuck in the far bank, much to the delight of the crew and some equally excited bystanders. An attractive reach of water now lay ahead that would remain with us all the way to Vicarstown. The canal is quite narrow here and at one point we met a traditional canal boat and only just managed to squeeze by. One wonders what happens when two of these boats meet in such circumstances.

We moored at Fisherstown Bridge for a short break. This is a beautiful little spot in a deep, wooded cutting and I could have quite happily stayed there for much longer. After a quick stop on the Grattan Aqueduct, we didn't let up until we reached quaint old-worldly

Vicarstown. This is the quintessential canal village with an ancient public house and warehouses which are now home to the Barrowline Cruisers rental fleet. The canal journey down to here and the small rural community is more reminiscent of something you might find along the Royal Canal. Perhaps coincidentally, I note that one of the civil engineering contractors who built part of this stretch was also the principal contractor on the final leg of the Royal Canal. For the latter (very large) contract, John Mc Mahon merged with the already existing civil engineering companies of Bernard Mullins and David Henry to form the consortia of Henry, Mullins and Mc Mahon. This was one of the first large civil engineering companies in Ireland and would equate in today's terms to the SIAC-Ferrovial alliance, builders of the M3 motorway. I wish to digress for a moment, if I may, on the more general subject of contemporary road construction and the amount of time now required to build these large projects.

Fifty years ago, John Laing built the 125km London to Birmingham M1 motorway in just over nineteen months. No less than 183 bridges were constructed with a work force that totalled over 4500 men, the majority of whom were Irish. It was a truly astronomical achievement. Fifty years later and despite huge advances in the capabilities of construction plant and equipment such a project deadline could never be achieved. It is easy to blame environmental issues as the thorn in the side of modern day infrastructural projects. Equally it is undoubtedly true that with an ever increasing importance placed on such issues, it is rapidly becoming more difficult to disturb the green sod of the Irish countryside. But the legitimate protection of our heritage is being abused by both sides. It's not reasonable that every excavation should be halted by the discovery of ancient human remains or disturbance to a badger path. With well in excess of 100 million people buried on this small island it is inevitable that no matter where you choose to dig it's likely that evidence of human remains or habitation will be found. But neither is it reasonable to wilfully deface parts of the countryside when there are other options available. However, this is all by the way and is incidental to the point I wish to make. Despite fifty years of mechanical progress, productivity is not increasing. Between the thirty-six hour week and a proliferation of bank holidays and the annual builders leave (that's almost as generous as that of the schoolteachers), machines are stationary an awful lot of the time. Site safety standards and regulations are being bureaucratically pushed to a nonsensical level that defies common sense. Just pause for a moment and consider, albeit hypothetically, the work output the early civil engineering companies would have achieved had they the mechanical resources of today at their disposal.

Vicarstown was our destination for now and it was a good safe place to leave the boat until time allowed us to begin the Barrow campaign. A taxi was ordered to bring us back to Glenaree. The driver reminisced – for the entire journey – about when Monasterevin became worldwide news with the 1970s Dr Herema kidnap. He was an ambulance driver at that time and played an important role – at least in his own estimation – in the recovery proceedings. Before we knew it, we were in Glenaree and it was with a little genuine regret that we parted company.

* * * * * * * *

The River Barrow is often regarded as the most beautiful of Ireland's inland waterways. But as with beauty, the beast is sometimes not far behind. It has a fearsome reputation with many boaters having at least one horror story to tell of their endeavours on the river. There are many likely reasons for this. The first that comes to mind is that, this is a fast flowing waterway in complete contrast to the stillness of the canal. There are few, if any, hidden obstacles in the canal; there are plenty of partly submerged rocks in the Barrow. But I think most people's biggest fear centres around one particular feature of river navigations – the dreaded weir. There can't be a boater out there who has not had nightmares about a weir. The very idea of them – a sheer drop in the riverbed with the water crashing over the top is, frankly, unnerving. With absolutely nothing to prevent you from being sucked over the abyss and to certain shipwreck is a thought that would freak out any reasonable man. For someone like me with an innate fear of water – along with snakes – weirs are best viewed from the safety of the bank. As the anticipated start date for the Barrow campaign was rapidly approaching, I decided that it was time to confront my fear of weirs. Undoubtedly the best way to do this was with a gentle introduction from the car window.

The first Sunday in June looked liked being the makings of a good day for a drive. Our children are now of an age that the very mention of the word drive sends them into hiding but my wife loves a Sunday ramble and so I thought it was a good opportunity to do a little Barrow exploration. A picnic was packed and we duly set off for Athy, where the Grand Canal locks down unto the River Barrow. As it happened, when we arrived, there was a boat rally in full swing, which I hoped might engender a little interest with the yawning people in the back of the car. But it also started to rain. Not just so much as a misty Irish shower but more of a Bangladesh-style torrential deluge. Each of the raindrops was big enough to cause a saucer sized splash on the surface of the river. Rather worryingly, this was to become an all too regular feature of the summer that lay ahead. But thankfully we were blissfully unaware of all that, on this freaky June Sunday afternoon. Besides all the weather forecasters, from Old Moore and the Dingle dolphins to the BBC, were predicting a scorcher of a summer. With such assurance of promising weather ahead, we were happy to put up with the misery, at least for an hour or two.

It's not possible to drive down to the first weir on the Barrow below Athy, so we set off on foot. I was getting a bit jittery and snappy about the whole silly idea. I could hear the water tumbling over the weir before I could see it, which try as I might, was becoming more and more difficult to ignore. This was the worst possible start to what was supposed to be a gradual introduction to weirs. My wife sensed my unease and she discreetly reached down for my hand (she's a little taller than me or maybe it's just her arms are a wee bit shorter) and squeezed it tightly. Despite my unease, I was glad of her discretion. It was bad enough for the kids to see their big tough macho dad acting like a toddler being brought to playschool for the first time. It would be quite another matter, altogether, for them to witness their parents holding hands. They have, quite rightly, never been exposed to public displays of intra-parental affection. Parents are embarrassing enough without that sort of carry-on and are, after acne, the second worst possible affliction in the lives of teenagers. I focused on my feet as we walked closer to the abyss. The birds were singing happily, despite the rain; the weir did not seem to trouble them. But what a ridiculous thought, I told myself – they do not venture out in boats that are drawn to a weir as summer flies are to meat. They can fly across with no risks whatsoever.

'Dad, look up, you're going to miss it. Look at the way the water is all swirly and white at the bottom of the waterfall – Dad?' Young children (aged seven) can be so innocent and so insensitive. Or perhaps I had put up a very convincingly brave front.

'Yes, I know, I can see it – it's, it's nice,' I lied.

'Dad you can't see it, cos you're not looking at it,' argues No 4, who isn't easily fooled.

There was nothing for it. It was time to face reality. It couldn't be that bad. I looked up, my eyes being directed by my ears. There was a lively, even boisterous, flow on the river towards the small waterfall. Within a short distance from the weir, the water became more glazed, calmer, more contemplative. It was as if the water itself was pausing to consider its plight. Then pushed on by the innocently exuberant body of water behind, it momentarily defied gravity and arched its silver back upwards and slipped effortlessly over the brink. With a rush of gravity-induced acceleration, the water fell vertically for a little over a metre. Excited and angry after its sudden release of energy, the virgin white water milled in the rough and tumble of the pool at the foot of the weir. But with the excitement on the wane and the lure of a good downhill race ahead, the water flowed onwards, seemingly quite unphased by the experience.

I considered what I had seen. There was little doubt that to sail a boat close to the weir would be frightening, if not downright foolish. The current above it did look quite capable of pushing a boat – my boat – over the brink. Equally there was no doubt that if a boat – my boat – were to cross a weir it would be positively terminal, certainly for *The Tom Rolt*, if not its crew. But, on balance – and I was now starting to rationalise my fear – given a reasonable set of circumstances, this was not awfully likely to happen. There was little need to court disaster and fly in the face of adversity. There was a generously wide settled body of water to the left of the swirling menace that invited safe passage. Not only that but the entrance to the canal cut, that bypasses the weir and terminates in a lock, looked familiarly reassuring.

There was little need to dwell any further on the hazards of man-made waterfalls, at least for the time being. The cut, overhung with leafy branches, would be an absolute pleasure to explore. (I should add that, at that point in time, I was unaware of the fact that the weir may continue along the side of the cut with excess water spiralling down into the river, in an intimidating fashion. But that experience was for a later date.) I had dwelled on the negative for too long. I had faced my fears, albeit from the safety of the bank. If I were a recovering alcoholic, I had gone for a whole day without a drink. If I had been confronting my fear of snakes, I had manfully looked again at that awful photograph we have at home of my son with a circus python over his shoulders. I had walked through the valley of death without even fainting. The voyage down the Barrow Valley would be brilliant with a bit of luck and loads of fervent prayer.

The second weekend in June was decided upon as the start date for the Barrow campaign. Because of the potential hazards of the voyage I thought it wise to have a second adult on the crew. Gerry, who had been on the Tullamore episode, was keen to come along. He had garnered sufficient experience on that outing to qualify for this trip. The third crew member (including myself) was my son who was, by now, the consummate old sea dog. And at the ripe old age of sixteen he was probably the most sensible of the three of us. He was the fellow who had called a halt to my foolish plans to travel up the Milltown Feeder where we would certainly have become as stuck as Shackleton's *Endurance* became in the ice. Thus the crew was quite suggestive of that entertaining Victorian classic book, *Three Men in a Boat* but we stopped short of bringing a dog. We had a potential candidate who was very keen for the position – a Jack Russell terrier – but they are very anti-social dogs who will pick a fight with their shadow. If their shadow won't co-operate, they'll fight with their tail. There could well be plenty of arguments amongst ourselves without the Jack Russell becoming involved and taking sides.

The few days leading up to the planned voyage were very warm and the forecast was set for it to continue into the weekend. If I may return to this matter of the public's perception of our Irish weather, I have long observed that if the weekends have good weather and though it spills rain, nonstop, from Monday morning to the following Friday lunchtime, it matters not a whit to most people. It still counts as a great week. An extension of this reasoning is also applied to the bank holidays. Reflections on the summer's weather are totally guided by how good (or bad) the weather was on the bank holidays. Thus the coincidence of three scorching bank holiday weekends but with relentless monsoons and storms every day in between, it still

qualifies as a brilliant summer. As a farmer and amateur weather re-
corder, I find this pretty irritating. Such people cannot understand
why the harvest remains untouched in the fields just because they
burnt themselves into a beetroot on the beach on a pet holiday weekend.

And this weekend was to be a case in point. In blistering June sunshine that had induced a frenzy of haymaking activity in the fields we,
feeling a little guilty, set off down to Vicarstown. But it is a great luxury to watch other people work, particularly other farmers, if you have
nothing better to do. However, this is very seldom the case. There is
usually some pressing farm task to be done and, moreover, has not
all work the habit of expanding to fill the time available? So much
so that it's difficult to relax. Say, for example, I had crop spraying to
do – or, worse still, combining – and we set off on a family drive on
a damp and drizzly Sunday morning. I would be delighted that the
Good Lord had clearly recognised my great need of a day off and had
removed the temptation for me to work on this Sabbath day of rest.
'Six days shalt thou labour' and followed by a wet seventh day which
is absolutely ideal from my point of view. However, if the day had
surprisingly blown up into a good drying afternoon and I spied some
lunatic combining a field – albeit at ridiculously high moistures – I
would, nonetheless, have to rush home and get cracking. The perceived opportunity could not be wasted. Distance would have some
bearing on this but not hugely so. Any field operation being carried
out, that I should be at, within 50 km of home is sufficient to spoil
my Sunday off. However, if I am further away from home, say down
in Munster, I can reason that I am in a different climate zone and
that it's still spilling rain back in my place. I suspect there are other
farmers with this awful condition but that it is totally unique to our
profession. I don't think that if a park keeper were out for the day
and he saw a colleague hard at it, that he would feel the need to rush
back home and start sweeping up. Or if a painter was off for a quiet

hour or two and he spied a colleague stealing a march on him that he would have to drive home like a maniac and get his brushes out. It's very definitely a uniquely farmer condition that is born out of a very competitive nature that seeks to maximise every opportunity that the weather provides.

However as we haven't made hay in years and the crop work was all up to date, I could go with a clear conscience. Upon arriving at *The Tom Rolt*, we filled her up with diesel – it wouldn't do to run out with a big intimidating weir up ahead – and loaded up our supplies. Donning our shades and headgear and stripping off our tee-shirts to reveal big white culchie chests, we set off for Athy which was a couple of hours away. Anyhow Athy is full of culchies (and Dubs) so three more wouldn't make any difference. The canal has been recently dredged along this stretch and it's a great pity Waterways Ireland don't do a lot more of it, as there are tracts of inland waterways that have all the navigation properties of a paddy field. It was very pleasant travelling down to Athy and at little more than walking pace, it provides a good opportunity for a lingering insight into the fields and farmyards along the way. A few years ago, when I were a lad, it was safe enough for one to have a good gawk into a farmer's field while driving along the country roads. But today some young spotty speed merchant is likely to round a bend with the velocity of Eddie Irvine and drive straight into you. The boat is now the ideal vehicle for this sort of hedgerow gawking and no better place than in an agriculturally rich area such as we were in, with the bog lands well behind us.

This time of the year is, to my mind, when the countryside looks its finest. The trees were bearing newly born and perfectly full canopies of luxuriant, fleshy green leaves as yet unsullied by the vagrancies of summer. The wildflowers are beginning to open their hearts and display their delicate colours to all and sundry. Insect activity is frantically feeding and breeding and multiplying to ensure that their future is secure. Bumble bees, though actively foraging since late March, take on a new urgency revisiting plants and bushes to check on any new display. Pollen is approaching its peak and the harvest of nectar must be gathered for the winter ahead. All of these creatures, like the farmer, must maximise their activities in a spell of good weather. The small hedgerow birds dart purposefully from bush to bush, swooping on any food that might innocently flutter into their path. The demands of parenthood have ensured that they must work all the daylight hours to feed their nest-bound young. Most human parents who have a SUV full of kids will be able to identify with this frenetic activity.

While it is far from being the most scenic part of the country, the crops in the large flat fields of Kildare, provided their own manicured beauty and looked to be full of promise. It was reasonable for their custodians to expect a very good harvest. Few other industries display the quality of their workmanship to the public in such an open manner. In all likelihood you probably have no idea as to how competent your non-farming neighbour is at their chosen profession. However, good or poor farming skills are usually quite obvious by a squint over the hedge. And in this part of the world, the farmers set a high standard. This is, after all, the traditional tillage heartland of Ireland. While there was hardly a decent field of wheat in Co. Meath prior to Ireland's entry to the EU, these fellows down here were ploughing in to the butts of the bushes and gaily threshing away. And now the autumn sown barley was approaching its most golden colour while the wheat crop was relinquishing its deep green hue for the lightest shade of yellow. The crops were revelling in the very hot afternoon sunshine which would greatly help each grain to be filled to perfection.

We reached Athy in the late afternoon, just as the Friday evening traffic was slowing to a crawl on all approaches to the town. Not that this would have any bearing on our chosen transport but we were anxious to move swiftly through the town for another reason. Very warm summer evenings tend to entice out all sorts of nasty creatures, like midges, wasps and hooligans. And while the first two pests are pretty universal wherever you might travel, Athy seems to have more than its fair share of the last category. It is a town that I am not terribly passionate about and it reminds me of some of the more mundane towns of Eastern England. Surrounded by very productive farmland, the town is an unusual combination – for this country – of significant agricultural industries and the influx of new manufacturing plants in the booming 1970s. The entire package is wrapped up in dated tile and brick veneer shop fronts which are hardly complimentary to the original character of the market town. But this is probably a very superficial view of what is certainly a very historic town commanding a prestigious location. And if you happen to live in Athy and disagree with me, then you are perfectly entitled to call me a foolish Meath man who can expect a good hiding the next time I appear around the place. But I have very nearly received one already – on a previous visit to the town.

Athy is, by no means, alone. Wherever the town, it appears that canals seem to attract disproportionate numbers of some of the more objectionable forms of human life. Urban railway tracks do as well but you are much less vulnerable to attack travelling at 100km per hour in a railway carriage. But plodding along an urban canal, you become a very slow moving target that is impossible to miss even if the assailant's aim is somewhat unsteady after consuming a trolley–full of cheap Dutch beer. And all the more so, this evening, when the heat will have induced a thirst of tidal proportions in those who are so inclined. With a few hours of drinking completed these undesirables would undoubtedly feel the need for a revitalising fresh water cleansing and start diving into the locks. This, as you will know, is not a particularly good idea after a heavy drinking session and all the more so if the lock is empty or indeed has a boat in it. But our passage was greatly speeded with the help of the lock-keeper who had anticipated our arrival. With not a little apprehension but glad to be through the town, I steered the boat out of the 28th lock and unto the River Barrow.

Such was my concentration that I scarcely noticed the lovely old stone horse bridge on our left. Its purpose was to enable the boat towing horses to cross over to the track-way which is on the far bank of the river. As we passed under the 1960s railway bridge close to the entrance of the first lateral canal (to bypass the weir where I had confronted my fears), we met a farewell party of yobs. In order to avoid a barrage of empty cans and bottles coming our way I had to travel closer to the wretched weir than I intended to do. It was a case of deciding on the lesser evil and neither looked very hospitable. But disaster was avoided on both counts. The consumption of alcohol had left the revellers better equipped to hurl insults rather than objects and we ignored the provocation in our wake.

* * * * * * * *

The Barrow is one of Ireland's earliest navigable rivers. The valley which it descends has long been an important trading route linking the productive inland counties with Waterford port. Its path was relatively direct and there is a steady flow of water throughout the year. Trading boats were already using it by the year 1537 when an Act of Parliament was passed allowing for free passage of boats through openings built into the weirs. It should be noted that weirs may be constructed for a few reasons. Many were built to enhance the fishing but more typically to maintain a sufficient depth of water for navigation purposes, especially at the low water times of the year. Equally weirs were built to provide a head of water to power a mill. Without the use of weirs, river navigations become unreliable and limited to boats of shallow draft.

However it was not until the Barrow Navigation Company was formed in 1790 that a serious attempt was made to improve the river's possibilities as a link from the Grand Canal in Monasterevin down to Waterford port. The engineers, Chapman and Jessop applied their expertise resulting in the construction of a series of lateral canals with locks, which effectively by-passed the long weirs. By the late 1820s, up to 50,000 tonnes of goods were being moved up and down the river annually. We were about to voyage down a river valley steeped in the historical roots of agricultural production. To travel the River Barrow is an opportunity to chart the turbulent waters of Irish agriculture over the past 200 years.

There was an important incidental advantage from the construction of these lateral canals. The latent energy of the falling water returning to the river could be very judiciously harnessed to power waterside mills. These mills, in turn, used the waterway for the transportation of (agricultural) raw material in and end product out. In this manner, the river and the farmland and the mill became as integrated as the three leaves of a shamrock. It is ironic that in these present days of high energy and transport costs that such cohesive and sustainable industry is no more. But sustainability does not necessarily guarantee viability. We live in a world were the lowest cost producer is supreme, regardless of the socio-economic implications.

Neither is there little new in this concept. By the 1850s the Barrow mills – as we would discover later on our travels – were already under pressure from cheaper North American flour flooding into Ireland. It was being carried as ballast on the returning emigrant ships. The natural advantage of these mills was being overturned by factors largely outside of their control. Not only that, but because of emigration, the market for flour was in decline. Equally, the cereal producers in the surrounding midland and south eastern counties were becoming exposed to external market forces like never before. The repeal of the protectionist Corn Laws which began in 1846 allowed foreign grain free entry into Irish (and British) ports. The firm of grain traders, R. & H. Hall are well known to today's Irish cereal farmers, not least our aforementioned farming friends around Athy. It may surprise some of them to learn that this long established company – which was founded in 1839 – was the largest wheat importer into Ireland in the second half of the nineteenth century. The sources of this imported wheat were little different to today; France, Poland, Odessa, Danzig and, of course, the three big grain exporters America, Argentina and Australia. Globalisation is not a new phenomenon; it's at least 150 years old. Neither is the concept of fair-trade. Today the term has become synonymous with Third World producers and indeed justifiably so. But it is very much an ideal and in reality there is scarcely such a thing.

Further down the Barrow, we would come across another very similar but present day example of the lowest cost producer winning out, with very serious implications for the local community. But, for now, we were about to enter the secluded and soothing delights of the first lateral canal on the Barrow.

14. Beer and Biscuits

⁂

Travelling down these man-made lateral cuts along the Barrow is reminiscent of the more beautiful stretches of the Grand Canal. It is similar to a secluded, narrow rural boreen with a canopy of overhanging leaves and branches. The view ahead is often limited due to the fact that there are quite a few sharp bends. You carefully edge around these with a degree of expectancy, unsure of what may lie ahead. On your right hand side, as you travel downstream, a stony island may just thinly separate the cut from the river below, as a form of continuous weir. Or you may well be removed from the river altogether with a wooded island in between. All of these factors combined with the snatches of blue sky overhead to give an idyllic, almost magical effect. While there are obvious dangers, the islands would be a heavenly place for children to play with simple rafts and swings and hideouts. For a young lad, it's real Red Indian territory and it wasn't difficult to envisage the white men taking a hiding from the natives and being forced to escape by water. But regretfully, today's children no longer seem to be interested in such playful and simple pleasures

– scalping the cowboys excepted, of course. I am aware that it is really uncool to tell today's kids about your own brilliant childhood – and indeed adult readers as well – but as children, we would have derived endless hours of fun from such an environment.

On reflection, I suspect that my own love of waterways may well have been initiated as a child. As there were no rivers or canals within walking distance of our house, my brother and I focused our nautical attention on a deep pond which was a short distance down the fields. When I reflect back on those days, I recall that we made wooden punts out of Smithwick beer crates, waterproofed with fertiliser bags stitched into place with a profusion of felt nails. But between a poor working knowledge of the Laws of Flotation and the ingress of water, each and every one of these vessels sank without trace. And all too often the crew went down with the ship. We would strike out courageously for the bank, frantically clutching at clumps of flag iris and reed mace. It was bad enough to be soaked to the skin but then we had to run the gauntlet by endeavouring to sneak back into the house, unseen. The pond was forbidden territory as legend had it that it was bottomless but we had, by our experiences, long disproved this myth. But we remained undaunted by our failures and as we grew older our assaults on the pond became more sophisticated. The adoption of more modern crop spraying techniques on the farm meant we now had access to empty five gallon herbicide drums. These we lashed to a wooden pallet (a much sought after collector's item, in those days) with baler twine which made a distinctly agricultural looking raft but one that, at least, floated. With the jubilance of the early Mid Western pioneers we crossed the 'great lake' unto new territory and claimed it as our own.

These watery exploits were clearly to remain in my sub-conscious. Around ten years ago I built a couple of semi-ornamental ponds in the garden. In an attempt to stimulate our children's formative play-ful interest in such things, I returned to my raft building days. But sadly, I was really only building them for myself. Such antics were outdated and could in no way compete with the football mania of the David Beckham generation or the Wii virtual computer games. So many of today's children's games are virtual but we preferred to do the real thing.

As we travelled down this watery lane, along the Barrow, we came upon the remains of the first of the riverside flour mills that we would meet. In a last ditch attempt to stem the tide of mill decline, Hannan's Mill at Ardreigh was refurbished in 1895 but it was to become silent within twenty five years and has remained so to this day. As we turn the pages of history in our descent of the Barrow we would come to understand, more fully, the reasons behind the demise of these mills. Once through Ardreigh lock we rejoined the river and meandered the short distance until the next lateral canal. The Levitstown Cut is the longest one on the Barrow navigation and is of particular interest. The river follows a contorted route at this point and the cut serves to straighten our passage. The considerable island that is formed as a result is accessed by a couple of quaint accommodation bridges, built to service the needs of the disfranchised landowners. After a short while we arrived at the ancient parallel lifting bridge in Levitstown which was lowered across the channel. This mechanical delight, which has a definite Heath Robinson look about it, provides access to Levitstown House and mill, which are situated on the island. When the imposing mill was operational this would have been a very busy bridge indeed. In the first half of the last century, the complex functioned as a malt house, despatching its end product by boat up to Guinness' in St James' Gate. It was a further example of an integrated industry that provided a ready market for locally grown barley.

In such a historic and atmospheric place, one could almost hear the horses and carts laden with sacks of barley creaking across the iron deck of the lifting bridge. By the 1930s, the larger and more progressive farmers – of which the neighbouring Greene family are a good example – would have largely dispensed with the services of working horses. In their place were tractors pulling much bigger loads across the bridge to the maltings. Perhaps a pair of pipe-smoking old timers leaning pensively across the half door of the nearby cottage voiced concerns for the strength of the bridge to bear these modern loads. But they need not have worried. The bridge was to far outlast the mill as a working example of these industrious days. For in 1943, the mill was gutted by fire, never to re-open again. The threat and reality of fire damage to mills was a continual concern; grain dust is a highly combustible and explosive material. Rotating drives and bearings can overheat due to excessive friction and so ignite what is, in effect, a tinder box. But with the tell-tale ugly blackening that follows a fire long-since washed away – the stately ruin of Levitstown Mill remains a proud and illustrious monument to a bygone age of solid achievement.

We moored along the bank – the Barrow has a chronic deficit of jetties – and Gerry wandered up to establish how to operate the lifting bridge. He poked around it for a little while and then began to wind a handle. After a few minutes of sweltering and seizure-inducing revolutions, he straightened himself up to view the state of the bridge. It had not moved one iota. It remained resolutely and defiantly solid on the stone parapets on the side of the canal.

'Yeah, you're an auld bollocks of a bridge,' Gerry pronounced his judgement on the bridge's disapproval of his efforts.

'Well, what's the problem, Gerry?' I enquired, 'you're not winding it fast enough. You need to build up some momentum.' Sometimes I just can't resist the temptation to gently tease someone who's already a shade flustered. I can be a bit of an annoying prat at times.

'I'll momentum you,' threatens Gerry, flicking a horizontal lever upwards, 'some thick Kildare bowsie left that lever down when it should be up.' Gerry starts cranking on the handle again and sure enough, the platform of the bridge began to quiver promisingly on the lifting chains. The pulleys overhead squeaked in protest but the bridge climbed shakily upwards, inch by inch.

'Now, Potterton, get your butt through here, before she collapses,' Gerry commands, wiping away the sweat off his brow in the style of Christy Moore leaving the stage. To travel under this elevated contraption was as risky as parking your car under the balcony of the flats on Sean McDermott Street.

'Gerry, there's no way I'm going under that guillotine. I won't be half way through before that auld ratchet slips and then it'll be lights out. Is there no sort of a safety lock on it?'

'No, can't you see there isn't a locking device? If you'd just get on with it, you'd be through by now,' retorts Gerry, clearly the worst for his exertion in the heat of the afternoon.

'That's all very fine but that bridge could be waiting to drop on top of me. It's like when you just had a couple of pints, you'd be sure to meet a guard on your way home. Normally you wouldn't be able to find one for the rest of the week.'

'Come on and hurry up, you're only making me thirsty. I'd kill for a nice cool pint, guards here or there,' responds Gerry.

However Gerry's thirst – or mine – was not enough to prompt me into moving. I then had an idea which I tried to run by Gerry.

'Gerry?'

'What?' Gerry snorts. He didn't look up. He was fiddling with something on the lifting mechanism.

'Can you look in the wood over there and see if you can find a big lump of a branch or a bit of a tree to jam the bridge up?' I asked, rather hopefully.

'What do you think I am – a boy scout? Feck it anyhow – I'm after pinching me bloody thumb in the ratchet. There is actually a locking thing-o-my-jig and its working now – come on, get cracking Potterton, you'll be dead safe.'

Gerry was right. My time had not yet come and there wasn't so much as a squeak out of the old bridge as we passed quietly underneath. But I didn't hang around to study its underbelly. The lock gates which marked the end of the Levitstown cut were straight ahead and were set correctly for us. In fact, all of the locks were with us down to Carlow; clearly the last boat travelling on the river was headed upstream. It's not nearly so convenient if you are following behind another boat and every lock has to be filled before entering. Within a matter of minutes we were once more down on the river. The sun on this gorgeous June evening was still very warm and with hardly a breeze out. It was high time to stop for refreshment.

Maganey Bridge was only a short distance downstream. We passed under the second arch of this fine old bridge to suddenly see a narrow boat – *The John Tyndall,* named in honour of the famous Leighlinbridge scientist – already moored at the jetty. I swung the tiller handle swiftly to the right to bring the bow of *The Tom Rolt* sharply around to moor in front of *The John Tyndall.* Gerry promptly jumped onto the jetty and held the bow with a line. But the river current caught me unawares and it quickly swung the stern of our boat in a compass arc out from the jetty. Before I knew it I was practically at a right angle as to where we should be. Quick action was necessary if our boat was not to be swung around through 180 degrees and facing upstream. I threw a stern line to the shore crew but it fell painfully short; we were fortunate that it didn't wrap around the rotating propeller. Thankfully I had already learned a tactic useful for turning the boat in a tight spot. As she was well secured on the bow line, I thrust the tiller to the extreme left and opened the throttle up which slowly but surely swung us back in an arc to the jetty. With the boat now securely moored and the excitement over, we closed up and headed for the nearby public house.

I am not a big drinker – this would hardly be the place to announce it if I was – but I have enough of an appreciation of alcohol to savour it when the circumstances are right. And as you will have probably gleaned, I have little time for those who over indulge. Moderation is good in most things and certainly where alcohol is concerned. My taste in such is very plebeian; I wouldn't know a good bottle of wine from a glass of jungle juice. Neither do I like the fruit of the vine nor any distilled product. As a result, the only alcoholic drink that I occasionally partake is the great black beverage of the canals – a pint of Guinness. Now far be it from me to endorse any product but I think it would be strange for anyone with an interest in the inland waterways to drink anything else. After all without the brewing activities of St James' Gate, the Irish canals would have become obsolete centuries ago. In Ireland, unlike in Great Britain, we had no coal mines or potteries or heavy industry worth talking about to justify their construction. Our waterways were really only dug for one principal purpose; alcohol brewing and distribution. The Irish canals were an efficient and, most importantly, reliable method of transporting barrel upon barrel of porter to satiate the incredible thirst of the country people. And for those who could afford it or thought they were too posh to drink porter, the canals brought them their uisce beatha – the water of life – the finest Irish whiskey.

Arthur Guinness would have had a complete monopoly on the canal traffic were it not for the earlier arrival of a certain religious sect. These people were manna from heaven to the fortunes of the Grand Canal Company. But their impact on Irish society stretched far beyond the hinterland of the canal. Without the profound influence of these gentle and distinctive people, we would have drunk ourselves into oblivion. Without the example of these people, half of all our waking efforts would have gone into growing barley to produce Guinness and the remaining half into drinking it. In short, without the efforts of these solid people we would have become extinct.

The Quakers, or more correctly, The Religious Society of Friends, are a religious sect with little time for the formality and structures of the mainstream Christian churches. It is a pacifist and practical religion which is based on good works and with a firm belief in the equality of all people. The first Quakers arrived in Ireland in 1654 and were to instigate a new middle class of industrious and hard working business people. It was really a case of needs must. As non-conformists, Quakers were excluded by the established church from a university education; hence few of the professions were open to them. In the main they were neither landowners nor farmers. As pacifists, the army did not provide any career opportunities so it was somewhat inevitable that they were attracted to the world of business were their drive and energy were put to good use. Quakers were devoted advocates for an honest and straightforward life with much greater emphasis on frugality than luxury. The consumption of alcohol – particularly the spirits – was, for a good Quaker, an abomination and tobacco wasn't much better. Mr Guinness would have starved as a young man if he was depending on them alone to buy his porter. And so steering their business acumen well away from the futility of the alcohol industries, the Quakers became involved in the production of another essential for Irish life – food, which takes a poor second place after drink. Wheat is the staff of life but it needs to be milled into flour to make wholesome and nutritious bread. This was the perfect business opportunity for these purposeful people. By 1780, many of the founding Quaker families were involved in flour milling and in other core industries in Ireland. These activities coincided with the inception of the Grand Canal and the dawn of a great new trading era. Several of these Quaker family businesses ultimately prospered to become household names, some of which are still familiar today; Odlums, Jacobs, Goodbodys, Bewleys, Shackletons, Perrys, Lambs and Pims. Across the water, their influence in the food industry was similar with such well known brand names as Huntley and Palmer and Carr's Biscuits and the chocolate manufacturing quartet of Rowntrees, Frys, Terrys and Cadburys. Incidentally, John

Cadbury, the founder of that firm, had a lifelong involvement with the Temperance Society and he began his business retailing tea, coffee and cocoa to offer an alternative non-alcoholic beverage for the drink-scourged working classes of industrial Britain. He could hardly have expected that his small and magnanimous venture could have grown into the huge company that Cadbury's is today. Other (Irish) Quaker firms endowed their businesses with similar benefits of their ingrained social ethos and disregard for alcohol; Shackletons, at their mill in Lucan, also operated subsidised tearooms to provide their employees and others with an alternative socialising venue to the public house.

The Quaker companies, both in Ireland and England, saw the business potential arising out of a linkage of productive farmland to water-side mills and utilising the canals for transport. Practically all of the Irish Quaker industries were located close to water transport and it was an essential attribute to their business success. Cadbury's, in England, used a distinctive fleet of chocolate brown narrow boats to collect milk from canal-side farms and to transport the processed product. Nor was it coincidence that many of these family companies were involved in similar industries and shared a commonality of business ideas. Comradeship and offering a helping hand to each other was very much part and parcel of their beliefs. To this end many of the Irish Quaker families developed trading links with their counterparts in England and beyond.

There can be little doubt. We, who appreciate and love the Irish canals, are indebted to the unholy alliance of Arthur Guinness and the Quakers. It is to these, very different, sectors of Irish business and their principal associated industries – brewing and milling respectively – that today's canal fraternity should be grateful. Without their patronage, the Irish canals would have become as obsolete and useless as a gentleman's folly. However, perhaps with not a little irony, history was to prove a little more generous to the brewing dynasty.

The Quaker milling influence, with a couple of exceptions, was to eventually fade away.

As we walked over to the public house, a happy group of people were seated outside, under a sun shade, making the most of the lovely evening. Inside and out of the sun's glare, a few men sat at the bar having a quiet drink after work. Some were perhaps seeking fortification to help them to return to face the rigours of family life. Others were probably there for the evening. They all looked up as we entered, with a momentary pause in conversation. We cordially nodded our acknowledgement, as it was obvious that we were correctly perceived as strangers in town. And while the premises are on the busy Athy to Carlow road, its more usual patrons were all probably very local in origin. Judging by the paucity of boating traffic that we had witnessed on the river so far, it was likely that the pub landlord received little support from the river. While the establishment was old, the building itself was more modern and there was an attempt in its interior to recreate the style of the old grocery shop-cum-general merchant-cum-public house. The landlord was of a friendly disposition and we ordered two pints of Guinness and a Coke for the underage crew member.

On such a glorious evening after a day on the water, the next few moments are magical. You eagerly watch the barman incline the gleaming glass and begin his well rehearsed and finely tuned pint-pulling procedure. He gently rocks the glass from side to side causing the dark liquid to swirl within, his right hand coaxing on the tap, while simultaneously returning the glass to upright. Hands and eyes are in perfect co-ordination. It seems to take an age. He firmly places the almost full dark glass on the counter to allow it to settle. Your expectation is rising extremely rapidly at this point. The stimulation is nearly over and the real business can begin. The now full and creamy topped and delightfully blackened glass is passed over, feeling cool, cool in your sweaty hand. The first sip is the finest. Like a child with an ice cream, I rudely send my tongue's folded tip upwards and outwards to sweep the creamy froth from my upper lip. It's good, it's so good. After a minute or two of silent reflection, we resume conversation.

'This would be a new experience for you, Potter,' Gerry casually remarks.

'What do you mean, Gerry?' I indignantly question, puzzled as to what was coming next.

'You'd never be in a pub at this time o' the day, just after work. If you stuck your head around the door of your local, the reaction would be something like when your man Silas Marner made his one and only entrance into the village pub. The whole place would erupt with silence.'

'Yeah, you're right, Gerry. And no more than auld Marner, I'm only realising what I've been missing.' Gerry had hit the nail on the head but I wasn't so sure about the comparison to the poor old miser, Silas Marner. But for all of that, Silas was an all right fellow – he was a sort of a Quaker – and matters worked out grand for him in the end.

After an hour or so of drink induced deliberation we decided that we would travel on down to Carlow. With at least a couple of hours of daylight left it seemed only right to make productive use of it. We returned to the boat and cast off into the Waterford-bound shipping lane.

The real intrinsic beauty of the Barrow valley was gradually unfolded in front of us. The river twists and turns and like a true professional dancer, only gradually revealing all her hidden charms. And like all the best acts, she would reserve her fullest glory until the end of the show. Being a quintessential river valley the surrounding countryside falls sharply to the river. The valley sides are, in the main, well wooded with the largest trees down on the river bank. Great willows, alders and oaks grow with their toes tickling the water, ensuring that even in the driest summer their thirst will be met. The deep rich alluvial soils of the valley floor sustain great heavy sprawling branches that reach out over the water. Thick curtains of leaves suspend from the willow branches to touch the water which gently caresses them in a form of perpetual motion. A secret watery cavern is created behind the natural curtain which begs exploration by those who are fortunate to have a rowing boat. In some places the cattle graze the water meadows right down to the water's edge. The river is becoming ever wider; the security of a narrow lane of water that the canal provides is long gone. We have become a small boat in a large body of deep flowing water. While the road follows high above us, the peace and gentle sounds of the river are all around adding to the timeless scene.

We entered the Bestfield cut, keeping to the left of the weir and the small island. On the Barrow there are defined boat-streams which dictated that on our way down to Carlow we must remain reasonably close to the left hand bank of the river. Below Carlow we must switch to the other side. With the lock in view we travel along parallel to the weir, which looks daunting with the water swelling over the top. But in reality there is little cause for alarm; with the rudder set full ahead and the propeller pushing hard, the boat cuts cleanly across the flow. With the lock behind us it is a short voyage down to Carlow. We passed under a large pipe gantry that crossed the river to the old sugar factory.

* * * * * * * *

The disembowelled remains of what was once the jewel in the Sugar Company's crown lay close to the riverbank. Similarly located to the mills and maltings that we had passed by, the factory's riverside setting was no coincidence. A ready source of water was necessary for the process and considerable quantities of its beet and sugar were transported in and out by canal boat. But it too, in common with the other waterside food industries, was to share a similar fate. Refined sugar could be produced elsewhere in the world, at just one third of the price of Irish sugar. Brussels had succumbed to the major worldwide sugar producing interests and decreed that a protected European market was no longer required. With the illness diagnosed, the death of sugar production came quickly. In 2005, Carlow – and Ireland – produced its last bag of sugar and the plant was closed. It was the end of an era that was hugely important in Carlow's recent history. Its loss to the whole economy of the area cannot be over estimated.

The sod was turned for the Carlow plant in January 1926. But it was not a completely new industry to Ireland. The production of sugar was deemed to be lucrative and attracted the attention of entrepreneurial individuals. In 1851, an innovative sugar factory had opened in Mountmellick, capable of processing 300 tonnes of beet per week. Mountmellick was a hugely industrious Quaker town and was known as the Manchester of Ireland. However sugar production ceased a mere ten years later. In the same way as American sourced flour had suffocated much of the native production, imported cane sugar strangled the pioneering plant in Mountmellick. There was a second attempt at native sugar production before the First World War, in a new factory at Sallins. However this endeavour is more notable for the fact that it was one of the first buildings in Ireland to be constructed from reinforced mass concrete.

The foundation of the Irish Free State gave rise to a new level of optimism in the 1920s. The Irish Sugar Manufacturing Company – which was privately owned – was set up in 1925. A site was chosen along the Barrow, close to Carlow town, to build the huge plant with its brick built chimney towering up into the sky. The town had an industrial past and was surrounded by some of the finest tillage soils in the country. In the autumn of 1926 the first loads of sugar beet were delivered to the plant for processing. A canal harbour was constructed to accommodate the beet boats which brought the roots from places as far away as Edenderry. Kinsmen of mine, close to that town and whose farm lay along the canal despatched their sugar beet for Carlow in this manner. But by the early 1930s the alarm bells were already ringing for the plant. The cause for concern was nothing new and no surprise; price competition from imported product. However then, unlike today, Ireland was legitimately empowered to protect its own domestic market from foreign imports. And this was very much the protectionist policy of de Valera's Fianna Fail government. This government was very anxious to develop a greater degree of national self-sufficiency from the tillage crops sector and actively sought the destruction of the extensive grassland farming that had become very prevalent in the wake of the Great Famine. The bullock and its keeper were seen by the political establishment as the cause of rural depopulation, emigration and everything else. The actual reality was more the result of market forces; since the 1850s grain production had become increasingly unprofitable and Britain presented a ready market for Irish beef. As a result of the Fianna Fail government's policy, many of the larger farms were broken up by the Land Commission with a subsequent redistribution of the land to smaller (ideally tillage) farmers. A return to tillage crop production was also seen as a viable way to increase rural employment and boost local economies. In this regard it was only partially successful. The national wheat area escalated within the Fianna Fail period of office but equally live cattle exports fell by one third, decimated by the Economic War, creating a serious trade deficit with Britain. However, sanity was restored to the cattle trade, to some degree, by the reciprocal Cattle Coal Pact of 1937. Increasing agricultural mechanisation allowed significantly greater tillage crop production but without a corresponding rise in rural employment. But with a commitment to its chosen path, the government acquired the troubled sugar factories in 1933, and they remained under state control until the company was returned to the private sector in 1991. With State backing the sugar industry prospered; by 1936 there were 28,000 beet growers, supplying four strategically – and politically – located sugar factories.

By the year 1976, the sugar industry was celebrating its Golden Jubilee. While the European consumer was paying over the odds for its sugar needs, the industry was flourishing. A farmer's contract to produce sugar beet was a licence to print money. The crop had very beneficial rotational benefits as well. Over 10,000 people were employed on a full time basis in the sugar industry, with a further 15,000 people employed in associated industries. The domestic market was almost entirely dominated with Irish produced sugar. Accession in 1972 to the Common Market opened very profitable and heavily subsidised export markets. The 1970s were truly the golden years not only for Irish Sugar but for the entire agricultural sector.

However, all good things eventually come to an end. By the mid 1990s the storm clouds were beginning to gather for the European sugar industry. Within the next ten years, a vicious combination of Brussels' decoupled reform of the Common Agricultural Policy and the short-sightedness of the owners of Irish Sugar sealed the fate of the Irish sugar industry.

As we sailed slowly by the once proud Carlow landmark, on that June evening, the plant was being dismantled before our very eyes. Huge excavators equipped with rock breakers tore at the plant's innards. Acetylene gas torches ripped through steel beams like a hot knife through butter. Massive fabricated steel rotating drums were craned unto low loaders awaiting a very dubious fate. It's highly probable that they were destined for reincarnation in a Chinese steel mill.

I was reminded of a chapter in L.T.C. Rolt's autobiography *Landscape with Machines*. As part of his apprenticeship, he served his time in a very large engineering workshop, building steam railway locomotives. Through mismanagement, the plant became bankrupt. But in order to honour its outstanding contracts, the cash starved company was unable to buy coal to fuel its furnaces. The once proud plant now faced an inglorious end. The great workshop floor which was composed of thousands upon thousands of railway sleepers was ripped up and thrown into the furnaces to keep the final steam on the hammers. The Carlow plant that we watched from the river was facing an equally humiliating and inglorious end. Like Rolt's former work mates before them, the Carlow plant workers and farmers watched in total dismay.

It seems that the Ireland of the twenty-first century would prefer apartment blocks and shopping centres to indigenous industry that sustained a great many families through hard times. Ironically, the great sprawling Barrow-side complex is worth more to its owners as a bare site rather than as an existing working factory. In the same way as Rolt's factory had to consume itself in the end, I wondered whether the European Union's high labour cost economy and cheap food policy will eventually consume us all.

15. Landscape Beauty

❦

A little care is needed to navigate the river through Carlow town. Once you have passed under the very low arched bridge it's necessary to cross over in front of the weir to the right hand side of the river. A short cutting appears, culminating in Carlow Lock. In keeping with what seems to be the norm for urban canals, this area was frequented by some unsavoury individuals who were carrying copious quantities of alcohol to a gathering down on the river bank. The menacing look of Gerry brandishing the barge pole was enough to dispel any ideas that they might have had. Gerry's very useful in this particular regard; he's so solidly built that I can always tell by the inclination of the boat where he is at any given time. But he has other useful traits as well and is good intellectual company; he shoots from the hip and the two of us go back a good way.

An unattractive riverbank apartment block has been built on what was the former site of the eminent Barrow Milling Company. This mill, along with others, had been run by the Shackleton family, who were a very prominent and progressive Quaker milling dynasty.

The family is probably better known today for its famous son, the Antarctic explorer, Sir Ernest Shackleton.

Once through the lock, the river becomes very wide and we could see nowhere that was suitable for a peaceful overnight mooring. There was now a degree of urgency as the sun was close to setting. After a short time we reached the entrance to the Clongrennan cut which suggested it could be just what we were looking for. It didn't disappoint and we moored at the jetty above the lock. We jumped ashore to stretch our legs but it was soon very obvious that despite the fact that we were only a mile or so out of Carlow, it was a remote spot.

'Jaysus, lads, we're in the arse hole of nowhere,' Gerry pronounced his judgement after climbing up the series of steps from the jetty to the top of the bank, 'I don't know where we'll get a night cap around here. Have you any rum or cider on board, Potter? I'll need something like that to help me to sleep on that auld foamy mattress.'

'No, not a drop, Gerry. I thought the' be loads of old hostelries along the way, as the boatmen were divils for the drink,' I innocently replied.

'I could have put you right on that. You'd be as likely to find a pub on Rockall as you would down here. Hey, see those lights over there?'

'Yeah, course we do, they're miles away,' I replied.

'No they're not, that's the Dolmen Hotel. We could walk over there for a few scoops.'

After wasting too much time debating as to how far away the hotel actually was, we then arrived at a unanimous conclusion that the barman would be pulling down the shutters as soon as we walked in the door.

'But we could get a taxi, couldn't we?' questions my son. He was clearly keen enough to get away from the boat and the two old lads for a couple of hours.

'Max, I don't know what kind of a taxi you have in mind but it would have to be a feckin' Hummer to get us out of here,' retorts Gerry. This was an accurate assessment; it seemed the only way to reach us was down a humpy track with a grassy spine right down the middle.

We resigned ourselves to the fact that it was to be an evening in, which was initially a little disappointing as were all looking forward to a bit of *ceol agus craic*. Gerry can play a few tunes on the flute and is actually very well known for his esteemed endeavours in this (artistic) field. As for me and my son, it would not be possible to find two more tone deaf people. We have no conception of what constitutes a melody and are, apparently, quite unable to even sing *Happy Birthday to You* to a recognisable tune. But for all of that, I actually like music. As an awkward teenager I had a notion to learn the piano – largely because my first teenage sweetheart was musical – and I began to take piano lessons. But I had neither the ear nor the co-ordination to be capable of even learning the basic scales. After a few weeks of this rendition, my music teacher was starting to tear his hair out in despair. The final straw came when, after a particularly difficult session for both of us, he told me in his unforgettable Drogheda accent;

'There's no hope for you at all. I think you have rigor mortis in your fingers.' Mind you, my girlfriend obviously thought that I had a touch of it as well, as she dumped me very soon after that.

Undaunted by having to provide our own entertainment, we settled down and told yarns and boy's jokes and my son who is a talented mimic, kept us amused. When the cabin lights started to flicker as the domestic batteries ran down, we turned in for the night. The stern doors were left open in the balmy night air with little fear of disturbance.

It was a beautiful and peaceful place to wake up with the soothing sounds of the river and chirpy bird song permeating into the cabin. I have tried to understand why I find myself so attracted to water in general and to rivers in particular. Perhaps it is something very fundamental in that all forms of life gravitate towards water, recognising it as an essential component of their very being. But that is a very deep hypothesis that does little for the average man. It's probably something much simpler.

I appreciate rustic beauty in its great diversity. But there are, for me, some essentials required to create a beautiful landscape. On reflection, many of these qualities are shared with the fairer sex. Form and contour are desirable, with flat areas yielding to more interesting undulating country. It's probably for this reason that I do not find bog land particularly attractive; it is too flat and uniform. Colour is a significant contributor to visual landscape beauty; contrasting rich deep colours that add vibrancy to the subject are essential. Trees and fulsome foliage and the adornment of pretty plants are highly desirable to a beauteous landscape; a scene devoid of vegetation is greatly disadvantaged. But there are exceptions to every rule. The almost shaven Burren is certainly not rich in woodland foliage or strong colours (alpine plants excepted) but is, to my mind, one of the most stunning places in all Ireland. And the musician, Sinead O'Connor, has a shaven head, but she's certainly none the worst for that.

The sum of these factors of contour, colour and foliage combine to create a classic landscape. The absence of any one of these attributes can be overlooked but the presence of just one of these qualities in isolation will seldom make a lasting impression. But the astute reader will have noticed that I have not, as yet, included water as a component of landscape beauty.

Water is the overriding factor in any landscape in terms of what it does for the beauty of the scene. The inclusion of water, whether bright and reflective or moving slowly and mysteriously, or fast and dangerously, is what adds life and beauty and vitality to the landscape. So much so that a vista that is devoid of the above three landscape qualities, can be transformed by the fascination of the water alone. Water is ever changing; we may not know where it comes from or to where it is going. It creates and carries a lively energy; we know little of what it has to flow across. We have no understanding of what's happening below its sometimes troubled surface and we can but ponder its often murky depths. Water is the crowning glory in any landscape, regardless of what else may meet the eye. And some women possess very similar qualities and present similar mysteries to the opposite sex.

We decided to travel on a little further before cooking breakfast. After a little early morning washing ritual in the river waters – similar to what the Hindus do in the Ganges except the Barrow is much cleaner – and followed by a mug of tea, we departed this delightful and sacred spot. Once we were through the lock it was full steam ahead and we had a glorious vista of water and countryside ahead of us. The sun was already quite warm and the lightest fog was lifting seductively off the river. My two crew members were chatting away in an animated fashion up in the bow of the boat and I was at peace with all around me. Rounding a sweeping bend in the river, a small country church stood in silent witness atop a lonely hill, whose elevated graveyard would seem to be of advantage to the more uncertain departing soul. Yet another sharp bend in the course of the river lay ahead – to be closely followed by the Milford cut – which I steered swiftly around, as always not knowing what to expect.

With a shot of adrenalin already pumping through my veins – like you might experience if you are suddenly awoken by a loud noise – I quickly pulled the throttle back. All that I could see straight ahead of us was the mother and father of a weir. The entire width of the river seemed to be taken up by this enormously wide waterfall. I shouted to the scouts in the front of the boat. They too were confused and a little concerned. All of my early worries about the awfulness of weirs came back with a vengeance. Had we missed the entrance to a hidden leafy cut in the riverbank and now were headed towards certain disaster? Why oh why had we not seen it? Those two geysers up in the bow were messing around instead of concentrating on where we should be going. There was no way that I could turn the boat around here; there just wasn't room; there wasn't time. Engaging reverse gear would not be enough to pull us back against the current. I could see the newspaper headlines already going to print; BARROW BOATING ACCIDENT LEAVES THREE CRITICAL. I had things already organised for next week and having both legs in plaster and a bleeping screen beside my hospital bed wasn't part of the plan. Who would drive the combine? What would Gerry's wife say – if she even knew he was down here at all? Indeed what would my own wife say, as she already thought messing around in boats was just asking for trouble.

It was Gerry who saw it first. Close to the edge of the weir and straight ahead, was an old arched bridge. It was partially concealed with overgrowth and ivy and was a good example of non-intrusive bridge design. There was a narrow stream of water underneath it and it presented a real alternative. Even if it was a watery cul-de-sac that ended up in someone's garden, that was fine. Anything was better than the weir. I set the rudder firmly in its direction and we sailed under the camouflaged bridge and into a narrow channel. But our concerns were soon evaporated; it was a gentle and safe and very picturesque little cut immersed in overhanging trees. It led to a lifting steel bridge up ahead and much to Gerry's delight, it was raised. A lock which was partially blocked by a carelessly moored boat came into view beyond the bridge. The scouts shouted out to see if there was anyone in but there was no reply. They were in there all right but in a very deep inebriated type of sleep. But the narrow boat's great strength is its width – you don't need a lot of room to pass by a sleeping and awkwardly parked boat. I negotiated *The Tom Rolt* into the lock chamber with all the skill of a delivery truck driver in a crowded Tesco car park and the crew set to work. It was time for breakfast and to have a walk around.

Gerry was the duty galley cook aided by my trainee son. The menu was to be comprehensive, with healthy portions of fruit juice and oat-en cereal followed by the traditional Irish breakfast. Why the humble fry is now referred to as such, I don't know. We, and most people I know, seldom had a cooked breakfast when we were kids and we were as Irish as anyone else. We usually had a fry on a Saturday evening complete with fried tomatoes, batch bread and big red faces. I'd say the 'Traditional Irish' tag was a *Bord Bia* invention to promote the bacon industry similar to those television butter adverts that lead you to believe (falsely) that a bit of Kerry butter is the best aphrodisiac you could eat. Lumpy porridge is the real traditional Irish breakfast but it's far too healthy and boring to get enthusiastic about. But as an oats producer, I must encourage you to try and reacquaint your-selves with this wonder cereal that's high in everything that's good (like fibre and omega 3) and low in everything that's bad (like fat and cholesterol). On reflection, the oats market is in dire need of a sexy advertising campaign – perhaps with your one from the butter ads delicately slipping a spoonful of steamy porridge into her perfect lit-tle mouth followed by the strap line 'Are you getting your oats today?' If that isn't enough to get you going, then I fear nothing will.

I went ashore while the breakfast preparations were ongoing. The hallmarks of an old estate – Milford House, the residence of mill owner, John Alexander in 1814 are close by with old oak woodlands and an adjacent enclosed stone yard. I resisted the temptation to wander off until after breakfast, which judging by the sounds was imminent. I sat down with my back to the sun on the steel crawler track of an old dragline excavator which was apparently still in oc-casional use for dredging the river. Such machines were a product of the L.T.C. Rolt era of solid, world class British engineering and the manufacturer, the Ruston Bucyrus company, was a very famous brand. These were some of the first cable operated excavators that ul-timately replaced the digging efforts of the Irish navvy. Such was the affinity between these machines – which were styled with a model number followed by the letters RB (this machine was 22RB) – and the navvy's shovel, that his simple hand digging tool became affectionately known to all and sundry as the lowly 1RB.

The sizzle and smell of frying sausages and crispy rashers is stimulating to the taste buds at any time. In such an idyllic location, it was mesmeric. A call duly came up from the galley to announce that the breakfast was ready. I don't recall why we didn't eat the meal outside as it would have made much more sense. The three of us enveloped the tiny table, so much so that it was practically impossible to eat without mistakenly biting someone's ear, which isn't very clever. However, sitting at a very small table, in a narrow cabin, with the kettle, the fridge and the sink within reaching distance is a great idea as you don't have to get up for anything. It was a good natured and unhurried occasion, washed down with tea strong enough to trot a mouse on.

Feeling very agreeably satisfied after the meal, we walked back along the cut to the weir. Despite our somewhat over-the-top reaction to our initial sighting, this is a very scenic sylvan place, well endowed with all the attributes of classic beauty. The river is teased out over a wide area accentuated by the island and the majestic L shaped weir. The banks are covered with deciduous trees creating an aura of great natural seclusion and privacy. The combination of old stone buildings and arched bridges creates an atmosphere of great antiquity and intrigue. But the bridge – under which we had escaped from the horrors of the weir – carried a reasonable amount of traffic for this time on a Saturday morning. The road ran parallel with the river for a short distance and then veered sharply left handed to cross the main body of the river on a much larger old stone bridge.

Once across this bridge there is yet another splendid old Barrow mill. But this was no ordinary mill. Milford was once the location of one of the finest mill complexes in all Ireland rivalled only by the mill at Slane, on the River Boyne. The local Alexander family built

the first flour mill here in 1790 and construction continued una-
bated until at least 1813. These were probably the golden years for
mill construction in Ireland, in terms of the number that were built
in that period. The great water-wheel – with a diameter of twenty-
two feet and a power output of 125 horsepower – was purported to
be the biggest in Ireland at that time. As an aside, some years later
the imposing Herdman flax mills at Sion Mills in Co Tyrone, on the
banks of the River Mourne, consumed a colossal 600 horsepower
supplied from four water-wheels.

By the 1840s there were no less than twenty-two millstones in operation at Milford grinding native wheat to produce flour for the domestic and export markets. Waterford was a convenient 85km downstream of the mill and was one of the principal ports for flour and
wheaten meal exports at that time. However, the complex was gutted
by fire in 1862 shortly after a refurbishment by no less eminent a
person than Sir William Fairbairn of Manchester. Fairbairn was an illustrious Victorian industrialist with interests in ship building, steam
boiler and engine manufacture and textile mill construction.

However, the fire was to be almost the final nail in Milford's coffin.
The flour milling days in this industrious location were drawing to a
close as the industry was slipping into a gradual decline. The repeal
of the Corn Laws during the Great Famine had opened the flood
gates to the extent, by the early 1860s, that Irish wheat imports ex-
ceeded native production. So much so that wheat from Egypt – and
other far flung places – was now wending its way down the canal to
mills such as Perry's at Belmont. These foreign grain imports in tandem with the use of more modern flour milling technology favoured
the development of large steam powered mills adjacent to the sea
ports. Boland's huge mill in Dublin's Ringsend, which was previously
operated by the Quaker Pim family, was a case in point; by the end
of the 1870s there were sixty-three millstones in operation there. But
despite these technological changes in the industry, for many of the

old milling businesses the end was nigh. Imports of cheaper North American roller milled flour were rising rapidly. Irish mill owners would have to adopt the latest development of roller milling – which was more power efficient – or go under. But flour milling was, within a few years, to be dominated by only the few who met the import challenge head on. Boland's Flour Mill had, by 1880, installed what was arguably the first automatic roller mill in these islands.

In the light of these industrial changes, other uses were sought for the Milford complex. A saw mill and a tannery were subsequently established and remained there for almost a hundred years. In the 1890s a water powered turbine was installed which generated electricity for the town of Carlow, bestowing it with the prestige of being the first town in Ireland with electric street lighting. Much to my intrigue and delight, a whining noise still emanated from the bowels of the mill building. This remains, to this day, a place of hydro electricity generation albeit of a low output, in today's terms.

In 1908 a pioneering water turbine was installed in Belmont Mill on the River Brosna to power the mill and additionally, with typical Quaker ethos, to light the homes of mill workers in the village. The mill's activities have ceased but a large modern turbine still whines away generating electricity for the national grid. And by the same token, the great Herdman flax mill is silent but the river's mighty energy is now utilised to power turbines that generate a significant electrical output of 850kw which is sold into the (UK) national grid. In these twilight days for fossil fuels, each and every available source of alternative energy is very welcome. The time-honoured principle of the water-wheel can be further refined to increase its efficiency for the much smaller (lower head of water) hydropower schemes. It is quite probable and highly desirable that the now wasted latent energy of the falling water at some of the old Barrow mill locations will, once more, be harnessed to produce power. There is also more than a little irony in the fact that it was principally the widespread adoption of the electric motor that led to the demise of water powered industry. Today the wheel has turned full circle and water derived power will undergo a renaissance to help generate the electricity demands of industry.

But there is no one single solution to providing the energy needs of the twenty first century. With no great fear of losing credibility I can confidently predict that small local heat and power plants will become increasingly important. As a farmer it is entirely conceivable that I and many of my colleagues will be producing a significant amount of our own heat and power requirements from energy crops in a few short years time. However the power requirements of mankind at large will never be satisfied by the output of very small local plants as a single bee is of little use without a hive. But effort combined equates to significant industry and thus the honey – and the electricity – flows to grateful consumers.

16. In the Heat of the Mid Day Sun

❧

We arrived in Leighlinbridge within a couple of hours of departing Milford. Once through the very ancient bridge – which dates from 1320 – the navigation reverts to the left bank of the river, as it was north of Carlow. As the river has a strong current through the bridge, it is quite difficult to cross the flow to moor at the quay on the other side. With the benefit of this information gleaned from our *Barrow Guide*, I decided that we would leave the exploration of the town until the return trip. This met with a small protest from the crew who wanted to stock up with newspapers and sweets and crisps and other good things. But they were easily satisfied with the news that we would moor in Bagenelstown which was only a short distance down the river.

Just north of Bagenalstown is Rathellin lock, which in keeping with so many of the Barrow locks, is an idyllic little place, with a very desirable old lock house close by. The cottage garden is within a former dry dock which creates a sunken and miniature walled garden complete with its own micro climate. Moving down the river, the very imposing old riverside warehouse with its multitude of windows stands forlornly as you enter the town. We moored at the very long quay and the crew skipped ashore.

Bagenalstown, in common with Tullamore, had in times past a benevolent landlord, Walter Bagenal, who had very grand plans for the town. But unlike Tullamore's patron, his plans were largely aspirational and the town albeit with a couple of very notable buildings, not least of which is the courthouse, bears little else from the Bagenallian period. This building with its six Ionic columns on an imposing site was previously visible from the river on the easterly approach to the town but the very recent construction of misplaced Spanish-style apartments has sadly obliterated the view. There are two splendid churches and while I am loathe to elevate one over the other, the cruciform granite edifice that is St Marys is a very significant building on a prominent location. The coming of the railway in the 1850s bestowed Bagenalstown with a fine railway station which is another architectural gem. And recent modern architecture has maintained the standard with a very pleasing glass fronted landmark building which is home to the Credit Union. It is a very attractive and vibrant town with a picturesque location on the side of the valley running down to an extensive quay along the river. The ruined Rudkins Mill on the island in the river has a stately old presence and was operated by the Rudkin family prior to their emigration to bigger and better things in North America. The lock – with a permanently raised swing bridge – as you depart the town is the deepest on the whole navigation and is a rather menacing claustrophobic place. Once more the latent energy in the falling water was formerly captured by the adjacent Lodge Mills and the mill race discharges its excited waters close to the end of the cut.

The seven arched railway bridge crossing the river further downstream is an architectural masterpiece, which should come as no surprise, given its parentage. It is the work of two of Ireland's greatest men, in their respective fields. Designed by the eminent railway engineer, Sir John Macneill and built by the celebrated civil engineering contractor, William Dargan, (both of whom had worked in England with Thomas Telford), the foundation stone was ceremoniously laid in April 1847. An estimated 16,000 tonnes of the finest quality local limestone were required to complete this magnificent structure. Dargan, in common with Telford, was the son of a small farmer and was born at Killeshin, Co Laois in1799. Arguably one of the greatest Irish born engineers, he returned to his native land to found his own civil engineering firm and as such was engaged to design and build a great many of the Irish railways. But his contracts were not limited to the age of steam locomotion; he constructed the Kilbeggan Branch line of the Grand Canal and also the Ulster Canal. He became enormously wealthy residing at Mount Anville in Co. Dublin and when Queen Victoria was in town in 1853 she called around for a chat and cup of tea. But Dargan never forgot his lowly roots – he declined her offer of a knighthood – and was renowned for treating his men well. I slipped silently beneath his towering stone arches in awe of its elegant majesty, remembering the poor souls who built it, undoubtedly grateful to Mr Dargan for the well paid work in the very bleak days of the Famine. Somewhat ironically both Macneill and Dargan suffered a change in fortune in later life and both sadly died in reduced circumstances. However, the contemporary Dargan Bridge on south Dublin's LUAS line is an appropriate piece of civil engineering to commemorate the life and work of this nineteenth century giant.

Within a short time we arrived at the intriguingly named Fenniscourt Lock, after which the river meanders its way through a deepening valley and guides us broadside by a very long weir. The opening to the equally charmingly named, Slyguff Lock – which suggests it is home to a wily old fox – is quite narrow but there is no cause for alarm. We hopped ashore while the lock was filling and stretched our legs amongst a secluded rural oasis of mown grass and leafy trees and old stonework. The afternoon was warm with all the scents of early summer and it was an altogether very pleasant experience. To have a cup of tea and a bar of chocolate in such a location adds to the sense of occasion and marks the place indelibly on your memory.

Some of life's greatest delights are very simple and of little cost. There is a popular misconception in the Ireland of today that a high financial cost must be incurred for all pleasure activities whether it is golf weekends or spa and beauty treatments in country house hotels or whatever. The springing up of expensive resort hotels in the most unlikely places all around the country bears this out. The same reasoning is also applied to most people's choice of holiday destinations which invariably must be abroad. When I tell people that we always spend our annual family holiday in this country, they look at me as if I should be the subject of a church gate collection, which I would have no problem with. But I wouldn't spend the proceeds being pampered in a four star hotel in Costa Fortune. Just recently I heard of a builder – from a place like Edenderry – who has personal holiday villas for himself and his family in several countries. It might be Bordeaux for this weekend and Naples in a couple of week's time and so on. His leisure pursuits must be costing him a very substantial sum and with a weighty and excessive carbon trail in his wake. I have no difficulty understanding why a person from Edenderry might want to get out of the place every so often. I'd be the same myself. But would not a simple little bolt-hole with a tin roof down in Ballyvaughan or Aughris Head be suffice? I realise that neither of these places would be renowned for their sunshine and that the breakfast roll would be a rip off towards Naples but is that such a big deal? Where has all this lust for scorching and cancer-inducing sunshine come from? And a breakfast roll is a breakfast roll, no matter where you eat it.

Perhaps I am, like the frugal, miserly and workaholic Silas Marner, losing out on all of this, but I still fail to understand this new life-style. Real pleasures don't necessarily have to cost a fortune and, on the contrary, are often free and in front of our very eyes. Where we found ourselves seated right now was certainly a case in point. There was pleasure enough here for anybody. With reluctance, we took ourselves away from this place but we need not have been too remorseful; there was to be plenty more little touches of heaven ahead of us.

The Ballyellen cut was soon in our path. Like most of these lateral canals, it is quite a narrow channel. I smartly rounded a very sharp bend only to be suddenly confronted with the open mouth of a very hungry looking mill race. This was quite scary to say the least, as the water was being sucked in with a pretty ferocious appetite. I do realise that there will be some readers out there, in the light of my tirade against lavish living, who would be delighted if the mill race had consumed me and my boat and puked the mangled remains out the other side. But personally I'd like to be around for another while and so I had to act quickly. I threw the tiller handle violently to the extreme left, while reducing our speed. Fortune was with us and the bow of the boat wheeled away from its lethal attraction. I made a mental note of this potential hazard for any future descents of the Barrow. The old mill workings have given way in more recent times to a lime works, which seems to be still in operation.

With the lock well behind us, the picture postcard bridge at Goresbridge was in front of us. Built in 1756, it requires no less than nine arches to span the river at this point. We would moor at the quay here but in order to do this it is necessary to pass under the bridge and swing a loop around the island and return up to the quay. Once safely tied up, it was unanimously agreed that due to the unaccustomed heat, liquid refreshment was urgently required. We walked up the town in search of a public house. There was an old establishment near the top of the street and we joined the local Saturday lunchtime drinkers. Perhaps predictably, there was included within this small gathering, the usual, semi-resident old codger who thought we were fair game for a free drink. We obliged but we made it quite clear that we did not require his company in exchange for our benevolence.

Feeling much the better of our refreshment, we headed out of the saloon into the listless heat of a quiet and dusty Goresbridge afternoon. We casually sauntered across the street, to be stopped quickly in our tracks. An open topped vintage car suddenly rounds the corner with very enthusiastic gusto. The alarmed driver squeezed his horn which emitted a quintessential Big Ears and Noddy type of parp-parp sound.

'Did you see that Gerry?' I ask, very foolishly.

'Course I did,' Gerry responds, 'sure he nearly killed me. If it's not a pimply little gurrier in a blacked-out fibre glass hatchback, then it's an auld lad in a wooden car with a cravat and leather goggles.'

'Which would you prefer,' I curiously ask, 'to get you? Like, if you had to choose?'

'That auld bollocks,' Gerry responds with great certainty, 'at least he might be insured. Anyhow, did you see the bird in the back with the big hat and gloves?'

'Yeah, did I what, she was alright', I enthused with a smile. In many ways, the ladies' fashions of yesteryear are more appealing to men, despite the fact that everything is securely covered up. It's a bit like Gay Byrne's theory that the best pictures are on radio.

'I wouldn't have minded a bit of resuscitation from her if I was on the way out,' Gerry states.

'Do you think she might have given it to you?' I mischievously enquire.

'What? Given me what?'

'The resuscitation. What else? Knowing your luck it would have been the auld fellow.'

With that a whole posse of vintage cars started to ascend the town. While I am unsure as to why they were travelling through Goresbridge, it clearly was something to do with the Gordon Bennett run as all the cars sported plates to that effect. And it was quite a spectacle. Many of the drivers and their passengers were attired in the finery appropriate to that glorious age of motoring. Old L.T.C. Rolt himself, had he been around, would have been in his element. He only ever owned a few motor cars in his entire life, two of which were the same make – Alvis – and both were built in the 1920s. He wryly remarks in his autobiography that driving such a smart open topped sports car as a young man in the 1930s presented a very dashing and debonair image. Driving the same but now very old fashioned car as an older man in the 1950s presented the image of an eccentric twit. But no more than the turn-ups on your suit, by the 1970s he was back in fashion and was seen by all as the coolest thing on four wheels. Incidentally the pair of Alvis motor cars have remained in the treasured possession of his family and are kept in running order.

However, old vintage motor cars such as were wheezing around Goresbridge on that hot Saturday afternoon, are like their counterparts of today, reasonably prone to breakdown. Despite all the advances in manufacturing developments, modern cars now let you down for much more trivial and annoying reasons usually caused by some idiotic computer fault. Computerised engine and car management systems are becoming far too smart for their own good. But we, as consumers, are our own worst enemies in this regard.

I, like the gullible clown that I can be, bought a Sat Nav for my car, which is an unholy mixture of computer chips and satellite tracking technology. It is potentially the most exasperating thing that you could bring in to your car and I spend my time arguing with the very pleasant sounding female voice. In line with Gay Byrne's theory, she's sounds like she's a joy to behold but for all of that, she causes me a serious amount of frustration. One afternoon, I decided to be guided by this lady – Sarah Sat-Nav – down to the boat in Lowtown. I already knew the way there, of course, but I thought I'd test her out as

Lowtown is not easy to find from our house. She was fine for the first kilometre or so. Then I was instructed to turn right down a country boreen which I hadn't driven down in twenty years. Everyone knows – the whole world knows – that this is the most potholed and God forsaken lane in the county. Not only that, but the arrival of a motor car was likely to frighten the natives and cause the cattle to stampede. I wilfully disobeyed Sarah Sat-Nav and stayed on my proven route and thought that's enough of that. Of course, it has to be said that the intervention of this very sophisticated lady could well be the lesser of two evils as reading a map is not one of my wife's strong points. Furthermore going around in circles and becoming ever more lost is not conducive to a harmonious environment within the family car.

However, Sat Nav aside, if the technology controlling the modern car's essential functions was used more sensibly the Automobile Association should have become defunct years ago. But our friends in the vintage cars had none of these technological worries. However, the very warm afternoon in combination with a bit of hill climbing and spirited driving meant the likelihood of the old engines over-heating was high. And in this regard the occupants of one particular car were not so fortunate. With steam hissing out of the radiator, the driver coasted the car into the filling station beside us.

'She's boiling.' I state, rather stupidly, to the driver who has just pushed his goggles up in disgust.

'Yes, it certainly is and before you ask, she's a 1924 three litre Bentley. And no, it has never boiled before.' The driver was obviously irritated by the attentions of gawky individuals, like us. But we didn't quite see it that way. If there was smoke pouring out of *The Tom Rolt* and she below in a lock, there would be plenty of gongoozlers gathered around to gawk down at us. A gongoozler is the canal's equivalent of a trainspotter, a sort of canal anorak who likes to idly hang around locks and stare at any activity that may be taking place. But they are a harmless creature and while I certainly show some symptoms of the condition, technically I am unlikely to develop the full blown disease as I am an active participant rather than passive observer.

'You may let her cool down for a few minutes and top her up then with water. Nip in and have a cup of coffee and we'll keep an eye on her for you,' Gerry cordially advised with not the slightest hint of sarcasm. He was only trying to help and he was, of course, despite his use of the female pronoun, strictly referring to the motor car and not the driver's lady companion. Gerry has a very helpful and decent sort of streak, sometimes.

'We shall have our coffee, but right here. Amanda, can you fetch the picnic basket?'

Amanda, no more than the hatted and gloved lady in the car whose driver had tried to kill Gerry, looked to be a very pleasant person indeed. Gently pulling up her full length and petticoated skirts, she slid off the buttoned leather seats with the grace of a butterfly leaving apple blossom in May. I recall reading that the sight of a Victorian ladies ankle, which was not normally on view, was a very exciting experience for full blooded males, at that time. Other than the face and hands, that was about all the flesh that they would get to see, at least on a respectable lady in company. It's a far cry from today when there's precious little left to the imagination. Anyhow, we got a quick flash of Amanda's ankle and it was very dainty and nice and promising. She smiled sweetly at her male admirers, probably glad of our presence. Were we not there, it's possible that she might have been blamed for all the faults of the 1924 engine and, furthermore, accused of the vintage run being all her silly idea in the first place. Wives, in the main, are so tolerant. They stoically put up with their husband's trying hobbies, female fancies, annoying friends and sudden adversarial irritability. Do you think that any man would be happy to accompany his wife if she had such a bizarre, time-warped pastime?

Amanda opened up the wicker picnic basket. Folding back the

lid it was immediately obvious that this was no ordinary picnic. It wouldn't have looked out of place at Royal Ascot or on the lawn at the Áras. Amanda had clearly put hours of effort into its preparation and presentation, so much so that it looked a crying shame for it just to be quickly consumed. It deserved to be delicately eaten, with a pause and a giggle between each nibble. Folk like us would appear as drooling savages when confronted with the temptation of such delicate delights. Out of respect to the magnificence of its creation, we must leave them to enjoy it in their own company.

'We'll leave you to it,' I said nodding at my two cronies who were transfixed by the contents of the basket, 'if you need anything at all, we are down beside the bridge.' It was highly likely that they would. The steam had ceased to spiral from the radiator but a dog-sized piddle of hot lubricating oil was forming on the garage forecourt right below the Bentley engine.

* * * * * * * * *

On our descent of the Barrow so far, we had witnessed the decline of not only the indigenous flour milling industries but also the sugar industry as well. From that point of view, it was quite depressing. The river paints a picture of a greatly diminished agriculturally based economy, with little or no integrated local production. This seems to be deeply ironic given the production potential that there is today compared to 150 years ago. But a rising tide lifts all boats and other larger exporting countries have come on stream. We have attempted to understand the reasons behind this phenomenon and have found the cause to be principally, but not entirely, lower cost imported product. However, there is one very notable exception to this riverside decline. Standing on the old bridge and looking back up the river one cannot fail to notice the massive Connollys of Goresbridge, Red Mills complex.

Connollys of Goresbridge celebrate their centenary in business in 2008. Founded by William Connolly four generations ago, as grain merchants and feed millers, the company then diversified into milling oats for porridge. The business developed steadily and with the passing of time, The Red Mills brand became a household name in Ireland and more recently, further afield. Their horse feeds are now exported to the United Kingdom and North America and greater penetration into Continental Europe is planned. Connolly's are a very successful seed and feed business that create a significant market for local and national grain production. With a turnover of close on €100 million and almost 100 employees, its contribution to the local economy is very important. It is refreshing to find such a riverside agri-industry thriving while all the others have fallen by the wayside. The business has clearly succeeded due to an innovative family firm approach and an impeccable reputation for consistently high quality products.

We departed Goresbridge in the late afternoon. The weirs seemed to have become bigger as we have descended the river and Borris Weir was the longest yet. The hot afternoon had brought a shoal of swimmers out to Ballingrane lock but they courteously climbed out of the water on our arrival and opened the gates for us. It was a real waterside family occasion with barbeques, beach clothes and children learning to fish. From what I have noticed over the years, most fathers of young boys seem to have an innate desire to teach their offspring to fish. I can only assume that it's a throwback to the hunter-gatherer days and fishing as such is now the only form of hunting freely open to them. However, my father would have no more taught us to fish as he considered it a ridiculous pastime. Neither had he any interest in other game sports. We were shown how to kill and butcher a lamb instead, which was altogether more useful and we didn't bother ourselves too much with fishing. I am very much of the view that the only place to land a decent fish is in the fresh fish cabinet in the supermarket. And as for eating lamb, I gave it up years ago.

And fishermen can be a peculiar lot. Despite the fact that they have been fishing for several hours and we are the first boat to come along in days, if not weeks, they insist on leaving their lines out in the water until the very last second. It's a silly exercise in brinkmanship in which the fisherman is invariably the loser. On our return journey there were dozens of fishermen out on the Sunday morning, all of whom were playing this game. I suspect the pressure was on for some of them to catch the Sunday lunch. My crew became bored of alerting them to the boat's rite of passage. One young man, with sunglasses so dark that he clearly couldn't see anything at all, was far too slow. His long fibre glass rod was cast out well across our path. His line went under the bow snatching the rod straight out of his hand. Thankfully for his own sake – as we were beyond caring – he was possessed of just enough common sense to release the rod when he did, otherwise he would have followed his equipment into the river. He became quite excited and agitated and roared a string of rude sounding words in a language we didn't understand. But I think he will understand what to do the next time a boat is travelling on the river. Maybe he should follow my example and catch his lunch in the freezer cabinet instead.

On leaving Ballingrane lock, Gerry enquired of the swimmers if they had access to a lock key to fill the outdoor swimming pool up again. The answer was negative, so we moored below the lock and our live-aboard lock-keeper returned to do the honours. I appreciate that swimming in locks is prohibited but on such a lovely evening it seemed a bit miserable to spoil the harmless fun. And it was very unlikely that there would be another boat along this evening. There was, quite simply, no boat traffic worth talking about on the Barrow that weekend. Over the three days on the water, we met about as many boats. We had it all to ourselves and the beauties of the Barrow seem to be a very well kept secret.

The river twists and turns relentlessly on its journey through Clashganna Lock – home to yet another old mill – and then we entered the Ballykennan Cut. This lateral canal terminates in a double lock, the only one on the navigation. There was a boat already in the lower chamber, headed upstream, with an entire extended family on board. Leaning, as I was, across the lock gates looking down into the chamber provided a great vantage point. Granny was quite old and a bit wrinkled and was wisely confined to a chair in the bow. There was a rope lying on the deck at her feet but I couldn't say if it was tethered to her ankle. But despite her slight excess of skin, underneath lay a bone structure that suggested that this was once a very fine looking lady. Her posture was still straight and upright and her hair still thick enough to resist the slight breeze. Her daughter and son-in-law were commanding operations with the help of the lock-keeper. Daughter had inherited her mother's looks. Now approaching her mid fifties, she was at her absolute peak and had all the appearance of clinging to each and every available product that claimed to slow her passage down the slippery slope of the cruel aging years. But my eyes – probably all of the eyes on *The Tom Rolt* – were drawn to the person who lounged on the roof of the boat. Probably about half of her mother's age, in her mid twenties, she was long, ultra brown, sensibly clad and perfectly formed. Her long hair lay scattered and strewn in thick full cords that framed her flawless face. She was oblivious to us, to the lock and to the beauties of the Barrow. She was like a rose of early summer soaking up the sun's energy and transforming it into a radiant beauty that would mesmerise all those whose eyes were graced to fall upon her in the months ahead. But I do hope she attained most of her wonderful colour on the Barrow and its environs and not in some far flung auld foreign villa.

17. The Papal Bull

❧

The Barrow from Ballykennan to Graiguenamanagh is possessed of quite the most spectacular scenery of the entire journey down from Athy. The river, wide and twisting, flows through a wooded valley with great deciduous trees rising from the water's edge to far up the slopes. No words of mine can ever do this particular stretch of the Barrow justice; I can only describe it as serenely beautiful and quite unforgettable. Our boat felt very small in such a context and while the breadth of the river may be intimidating, its actions were gentle and reassuring. To walk along the Barrow Way – the track-way which faithfully accompanies the river all the way down from Athy – must be one of the most delightful walks in the country, east of the Shannon. It is maintained in excellent order by Waterways Ireland. I should love to walk it in its entirety at some later stage in my life when time allows such pleasures.

We rounded a long sweeping bend and our destination was in sight. Lines and lines of boats – of all shapes and sizes – lay moored along both sides of the great river. But sadly Graiguenamanagh was to be the end of our journey for now. We had decided to start the home-ward voyage the next morning. St Mullins was only a couple of hours further down the river – after which it becomes tidal – but I was anx-ious to return up to Leighlinbridge by the next evening. We would leave the boat there awaiting the final leg of the return journey, at a later date.

After mooring *The Tom Rolt* along the old quay wall, we gladly set foot on *terra firma* to walk into the town. An Irish couple on a narrow boat moored beside us had spent a lovely sunny week down here with their two small chirpy children and they were all as brown as berries. Being a Saturday evening there was quite a buzz about the place with activity on many of the boats moored along the bank. Ogling other people's boats is a popular pastime within the boating community. To anyone else it's about as exciting as shopping on-line for a toilet seat or wallpaper. I could happily while away an hour or two perusing a goodly selection of craft. But my interest is much more universal than that – it's not just confined to the small inland stuff. Whenever we are out and about, on or near the coast, a visit to a port or harbour is essential. One day, a couple of years ago, we were down on the Shannon Estuary and we ended up in Foynes. I spied a bit of shipping activity and I left my normally reticent wife happily ensconced with a newspaper in the car. Two hours later she was well informed on national and world affairs. After three hours she had the Crosaire crossword (the complex one) completed. After four hours she was hopping mad. The trouble was, I knew nothing at all about this and I very innocently wandered back into a lion's den when they had finished unloading the banana boat.

Our first requirement in Graiguenamanagh was a substantial evening meal. A promising looking restaurant was found and we felt sufficiently tempted by the displayed menu to occupy a window ta-ble. Unfortunately eating out can be, all too often, a very disappoint-ing and expensive waste of time and one is reluctant to commit to an unknown establishment without so much as a personal recommendation. Soup of the day – homemade cream of mushroom with croutons – followed by medium rare twelve ounce sirloin steaks (with all the trimmings) was the popular choice of our ravenous little party. And what better way to accompany red meat than with a pint of the black stuff. With all this inside you, you're fit for anything. You feel good through and through and you know the whole world is smiling with you. And the meal, happily, was reasonably satisfactory. But this could be interpreted as high praise indeed for the restaurant as I am very particular about my red meat. As already suggested, I no longer care for lamb but I am wildly passionate about beef. I look at beef animals on the hoof and longingly consider their virtues on the table as other men expound the virtues of a super car or a super model. I am reminded of my younger days when there were much more cattle than corn on the farm. On a summer Saturday morning the cattle yard would be milling with maybe a couple of hundred Hereford cross bullocks rounded up for a time-honoured weekly ritual. My father would walk carefully through them, ash plant in hand, selecting the fat animals for next week's market. My brother and I would follow shuffling along behind acting as drovers to draw off the chosen steers. The old herd, Carr, would be in a commanding position at the drawing gate which was at the top of the yard;

'Here, laddie, there's a good auld bullock – that great big black whitehead over there with his arse to the chute,' my father would order, 'he's mad fit. He should have been gone months ago, I don't know how I missed him. Drive him up slowly to Carr there, nice and handy, along the outside.'

Carr was watching everything that was going on, with the vigilance of a hawk hovering over a hedgerow.

'You may leave that bullock there, Boss,' Carr would shout to us, down the yard, 'don't touch him.'

'Why? He's as fit as ever he's going to be. Sure he has a full mouth.

Let him up.' The Boss wasn't having any of it. The full mouth was a reference to the fact that the bullock was at least five years old. No self-respecting beef animal today would allow himself to become this old. He'd be as tough to eat as a Killorglin mountain goat. Most beef animals are now slaughtered at in or around thirty months old.

'You may leave him alone. Anyhow he's not yours and you needn't be lookin' at him.' Carr was in no humour for debate.

'And whose is he?' Dad would question the validity of Carr's judgement. Furthermore his ownership of most things was not usually brought into question.

'That's Father Mc Grath's bullock.'

In those days, pre the advent of cattle passports and herd numbers and all the rest of today's regulations, many farmers fed a few cattle for the local parish priest. But we always seemed to have far more than our fair share. On a really frustrating Saturday morning, my father would have to leave every other bullock that caught his eye. On such a day, Father Mc Grath seemed to own at least half the fit cattle in the yard, each one better than the last. But, of course, the priest's cattle always stuck out as the pick of the bunch because they had been with us for years as the good man of faith had little time or use for mammon. But EU regulations put a stop to the practice and anyhow once Carr had retired, I think the sacred herd was unintentionally sacrificed. Besides, it would be a foolish man who would invest the parochial denarii in beef cattle today, as it would require nothing short of a miracle to make money out of them. The Irish beef industry is now facing its biggest ever challenge from cheaper South American imports since the first refrigerated ships sailed up into the Northern Hemisphere in the 1880s. And as we have already witnessed the political betrayal of the European sugar industry, anything is possible. And that could include the elimination of Irish beef production.

I expect it is as a result of this lifetime of exposure to walking meat that I would prefer to eat the boiled tongue of an ox or a sheep's bladder rather than be subjected to a poor steak. Equally a good (Irish) steak or roast is, in my opinion, the finest food a person can eat. How a vegetarian can resist the temptation of such a main course is beyond me. All this stuff about the morality of raising and slaughtering animals for food is balderdash. If there is such a thing as reincarnation, I am more than content to come back as a beef animal, ideally as an apostolic bull. It'd be a great life and I would certainly die happy. I am long of the view that if my own passing is as painless as that of a humanely slaughtered animal, there's nothing to worry about. Sadly many human beings have to face much more traumatic and distressing final moments.

As dusk was falling in Graiguenamanagh, sadly time did not allow for a walk up to the Cistercian Abbey. I find myself drawn to such historically rich old sites of simple Christian living and of deep learning, in the fervent hope that a little of it might seep into me. These early monastic communities were the true Celtic people and the qualities of their lives are so desperately different to ours of the Ireland of today. To spend a little quiet and reflective time walking around these great monuments is always enriching and it's not difficult to imagine the hive of earnest activity that these places were in ancient days. Clonmacnoise is a very fine example of such a place and I hope to travel there by water at some stage.

I woke early on the Sunday morning. We had slept with the stern doors open and I could see that the river was enveloped in a thick fog. The interior of the cabin was slightly foggy too but whether it was related to that outside, I couldn't say. Either way, it should be well disappeared before the rest of the crew surfaced. It seemed incredible to have such an autumnal feature in June but Gerry who knows about such things, later explained that a combination of water and the deep valley would give rise to a micro climate, quite different to anything we might experience at home. After a discussion on this and other less taxing matters, we eased ourselves out of bed and gradually got the day rolling. The fog was beginning to clear outside and it was but a memory by the time we were ready to turn for home. It was a lovely early summer morning but there was more cloud beginning to gather than in recent days. We were swiftly through the locks and before we knew it, we were up to Goresbridge where we stopped for some lunch. We didn't delay for long as there was a fair journey still ahead of us. It was evening by the time we arrived back in Leighlinbridge where we moored at the old quay. We were becoming tired of relaxing at this stage and, in truth, glad to mooring up. Too much leisure time becomes stressful and three full days on the trot is quite long enough. But the weekend's journey had been a good success with scarcely a dull moment and no mishaps which was somewhat unusual.

I had the phone number of a taxi which we had used before, to bring us back to the jeep – which was up in Vicarstown – but he was unavailable. Faced with a dilemma, we discussed how we would locate any other taxis around.

'Tell you what,' said a grinning Gerry, clearly pleased with his rush of genius, 'if you run up to the hotel and ask in reception. They'll tell you about the taxi men, around here.'

Nobody had a better idea, so I headed off up the town. The receptionist looked somewhat disdainful as I crossed an acre of marble floored lobby to reach her magnificent marble and glass throne. I caught a glimpse of my reflected self in the gleaming plate glass. I hadn't realised it but I did look a bit scruffy. She wasn't very happy with me at all.

'Yes, can I help you?' she curtly asked, in an ice cold voice. I was a bit put out by this. I wasn't going to attack her.

'Yes you can. I'm looking for a taxi. Do you have the number of any, please?' I replied.

'Where do you want to go to?' The ice maiden enquired. I felt that this was irrelevant as far as she was concerned.

'Home,' I replied.

'Where's that?' She persisted.

'Up the country,' I retorted, 'I only want his number – please.'

'Shall I order you a taxi?' she enquired.

'No, the number please. I need to do a deal with him, before he leaves his base – otherwise he might rob me,' I explained.

I meant that he might charge me an excessive amount for the 70 km round trip in the absence of an agreed price beforehand. I didn't want to be stung for a hundred euro getting out of the cab when I would have little choice but to pay up. My icy friend clearly misunderstood me.

'There'll be little fear of that – it's him, I'd be worried about.' The ice maiden quipped, pushing a scribbled number across the marble counter with an outstretched arm, her body staying exactly where it was. The note was still a little way off. She clearly had a pre-conceived notion about me, so I thought I'd better play to the gallery.

'You'd hardly mind if the missus and the childer came in for a few hours 'till I get back with me Hi Ace,' I enquired, making a lunge for the note.

I didn't wait for the reply. With all the unease of Crocodile Dundee in New York, I beat a hasty retreat across the great marble atrium and back to the grubby old boat. And in fairness to the receptionist when I related my experiences to the guys, they nearly split themselves with laughter.

'What's so funny?' I asked, all indignant.

'Look at the state of you, Potterton,' Gerry puts me wise. 'You are an unshaven grease monkey with your fly at half mast, on a Sunday afternoon. What sort of welcome did you expect – afternoon tea with her in the lobby? If I was her, I'd have called the guards.'

I looked down at myself. Somewhere, somehow, since morning I had come into contact with the finest of black lock grease. It was smeared all over the front of my jeans. I ran my fingers over my face. I was, as the children would say, all jaggy. Gerry was right. I was no beauty. And they knew it when they sent me up on the errand.

* * * * * * * * *

It was a couple of weeks before we returned to *The Tom Rolt* in Leighlinbridge. The weather had greatly deteriorated, into the awful summer that it had become, with scarcely a fine day since that smashing June weekend. Early on a Saturday morning with a reasonably promising weather forecast, we met up in Vicarstown. The crew comprised the three of us, as before, plus Gerry's daughter, who is a similar age to my fellow. The plan was to leave one vehicle in Vicarstown and all go down together to the boat. That way we would eliminate the need for a taxi, on our return. The food supplies for the day were loaded up along with a few drums of diesel for the boat. We found everything as we had left it on *The Tom Rolt*; the good people of Leighlinbridge had kept her safe.

With all gathered up and under a fleeting sky we crossed over to the far side of the river and passed beneath the old bridge. Due to all the rainfall in the interim, the river was a lot higher and faster than previously. Besides, this reach of water is noted for its fast current at the best of times. But at a couple of places along the way, such was its force that we were scarcely moving forward at all. The Kubota engine – which had performed faultlessly since its installation – was working extremely hard and I had concerns that the journey would take an absolute age. On the bank, keen walkers well wrapped up against the head wind, battled on ahead of us, smiling sympathetically as they passed. We just grimly nodded. We didn't think there was a whole lot to smile about as travelling upstream in such conditions is very testing on patience and stamina. Some months later on, a friend who lives aboard in Lowtown told me of his similar experience. He bought a narrow boat in August – which was a notoriously wet month – down in Graiguenamanagh and he gaily set off for distant Lowtown but progress was so painfully slow that he abandoned ship in Bagnelstown. He had the boat lifted out of the water there and brought up by road on a flatbed truck.

With the increased flow the weirs were much more menacing and I regretted that I hadn't got an anchor on board. At times like this, worries do not just come in singles but in multiples to erode any sense of well being that you might have. But the lack of an anchor was very foolish. With a strong current close to a weir an anchor could prevent the situation getting out of control.

Thankfully the very dark clouds of life usually give way to a little brightness in time, which is just sufficient to keep the spirits up. By mid morning progress had improved considerably and the absolute snail's pace of Leighlinbridge was not repeated. But care was needed, particularly when entering a cut. Where the waters meet, the flow was fast and aggressive and often meeting our bows obliquely. This had the effect of pushing the boat unto the river bank and it was quite a battle with the rudder to hold our direction. It was a steep learning curve and the occasional rocks jutting treacherously out of the bank provided a cautionary incentive. To add to the difficulty, as we were locking ourselves through, it was necessary to moor below the lock to put a man ashore. Again the current made this much more awkward than on our downriver voyage. But I had confidence in our engine to hold to our course and in this regard we were certainly not disappointed.

As we entered Carlow lock, despite it being a Saturday morning, a gang of Waterways Ireland workers were repairing the security meshes on a building close to the lock. It was obviously deemed enough of a priority to muster the forces into overtime. And given the aforementioned area we were in this was understandable. A supervisor monitored progress but he presented an air that he was much too busy to engage in conversation. While the manpower required to do the job looked to be excessive – which is inevitable with a State organization – the quality of work generally carried out by Waterways Ireland has improved very considerably. Having said that, a recent walk along the Royal Canal near Thomastown, revealed new repairs in mass concrete to a beautifully inverted old stone culvert. The engineer who sanctioned this crudely utilitarian work should be disgusted with his efforts. The day and age of this type of vulgarity has long since passed.

We lunched at Bestfield Lock – which takes its name from the family of A. Caulfield Best Esq who lived nearby in 1814 – and this was a relaxed affair with coffee and rolled bread. The day was now showery but we had been fortunate enough so far and were graced with pleasant sunshine for the break. Our *Barrow Guide* informed us that this lock is reputed to be haunted but we should be safe enough from any supernatural forces on a June afternoon. That said, nothing would persuade me to spend the night there. There are quite enough strange noises on a boat at night to convince me that it's a poltergeist's heaven. I would be a complete wimp in this regard and accredit this to the fact that I was born in a haunted house. My mother who, like my wife, is very relaxed about such matters, freely admits to hearing the piano play (tunefully) by itself in the wee small hours, when we were children. Part of my own house is very old and under no circumstances would I sleep up in the ancient part on my own. But what irritates me most about this sort of thing is that I seldom hear anything unusual until I am all alone (so far as I know) in the house. Then I can rest assured that all hell will break loose. Pictures will slide down the wall, window weights will drop and the stairs will creak as though it was as busy as that in a nightclub. Nothing ever happens when the house is full of (living) people. Alone, with no one to ask or confirm that they too heard the commotion, I become a sweaty nervous wreck for the remainder of the night.

L.T.C. Rolt had an interest in the supernatural world and wrote two or three books concerning haunted canal locks and the like. But I haven't read them as so far as I am concerned the less you know on this sort of thing, the better. I shall leave the final words on the matter to an old man who worked on the farm when we were children.

'Johnny,' we would ask the old man while he toothlessly munched his way through a hard cheese doorstep of a sandwich for his lunch, 'would you be afraid if you heard a ghost in your house at night?' It should be noted that Johnny was a bachelor with a great gra for the demon drink and it was very unlikely that he would hear anything short of an earthquake once he retired for the night.

'Naw, it's the fellow who is alive that I would be more afeared of.'

In the Ireland of today where a human life is so often violently taken and long after Johnny has been laid to peaceful rest (I have no reason to believe otherwise) these words were never more apt.

Within a short time we were back up at Maganey Bridge but we didn't delay as there was a still a good way to go and the day was pressing on. Gerry was ultra competent with the workings of Levitstown lifting bridge – perhaps a bit too cocky – but we were soon speedily and safely under it. By this time, the evening had become extremely damp and showery which made it ideal for the journey through Athy. The hooligan element were not to be seen and had presumably retired to drown their sorrows in an unoccupied warehouse or the like. We were soon on the last leg of the return journey up to base camp Vicarstown.

18. In Female Company

⸺

The Tom Rolt lay in Vicarstown for a couple of weeks before we took her up to Lowtown. On one memorable Saturday morning, my youngest daughter – aged seven and who loves a day out on the water – and I decided that we would start the journey back to base. The plan was to bring the bike with us on the boat and then we would cycle back to collect the jeep to return home. We loaded up our stuff and departed Vicarstown in warm sunshine. In the fields the winter barley crops were beginning to droop their golden heads which is a clear indication that the harvest is nigh. My boating days would soon be few and far between for the next two months. But it was good to be out while there were still some guilt-free days of leisure still remaining.

I particularly like this stretch of the canal; it's very pleasant countryside with a nice mix of trees and hedgerow along the waterway. We crossed over the Grattan Aqueduct but didn't stop as there would be ample opportunity when cycling back along the towpath. But I was puzzled by the linkage of this aqueduct to a very illustrious Irish family and resolved to research the matter when we returned home. The family of Henry Grattan, statesman, orator and leader of the patriot parliament have a long connection with Co Laois. Dunrally Castle which lies in ruins on the banks of the Barrow close to Vicarstown was once the home of this eminent man. In fact he was so taken with the place that he expressed a wish to be buried there. However, upon his death, someone else decided that he would be better off in Westminster Abbey and since he wasn't in a position to argue, that's where he ended up. As a very distinguished local landowner it is only right and proper that the aqueduct – which was built in 1790 – bears his name.

There is, at least, one other place that should quite rightly be associated with Henry Grattan. The surrounding land and the farm on which I live was, in former days, owned by Grattan and a branch of my family were in fact tenants of his. But the land slipped through their hands and into those of our (extended) family. However between an unholy combination of slow horses, fast women and beef in the winter, we also were forced to relinquish ownership something over a hundred years ago. But happily we were restored, as they say, in more recent times. Moving on in the years, our local village was not immune to the Celtic Tiger building boom whereby its population increased about five-fold and names were sought for the new housing estates. I eagerly suggested such names as Grattan Park and Grattan's Grove for the standard type housing estates, reserving Grattan Court for the really upmarket double garage, triple en-suite developments. But the County Council had its own ideas and instead opted for the more mundane. Regrettably, the Grattan connection with the village and locality remains a curiosity for most people.

From Courtwood Bridge to Fisherstown Bridge the canal travels through a deep cutting which is a lovely stretch of water. My travelling companion and I thought this would be a nice place to moor the boat for a while and have a chat. We would then decide as to whether to go on any further or leave the boat here until the next time. Children love coming on the boat as it's like a play house that floats around and into which adults are welcome. The two of us had a special time; my little friend played house with a couple of live–aboard Bratz dolls who – rather surprisingly – love their life on the water while I sat in the bow with a book. While there is undoubtedly plenty of space for two dolls to take up residence, I think it's more adequate than that.

There is something very appealing and comfortable about the living accommodation on board a narrow boat. Some people of a cynical mind might refer to them as having all the space and shape and comforts of a coffin but in reality it's not like that. Narrow boats are ergonomically designed to maximise the living space available and it's a form of minimalist living. Many people today – my own family very definitely included – fill their houses up with unnecessary clutter. As we live in such a consumer, shop-till-you-drop society, a great many people increasingly spend their Saturdays shopping for what they have little need. Then they return wearily and financially lighter to their homes with a SUV full of expensive flat pack junk and with nowhere to put it. Failing to understand the problem, they convince themselves that it's a bigger house that's required. Junk has a habit of expanding to fill the space available. *The Tom Rolt* has approximately 250 square feet of living space, which is shade smaller than a one bedroom city apartment. I see little reason why two intimate people could not comfortably live on such a floor area on a permanent basis. However if you happen to have a disagreement with your boat mate whether transitory or more long term, it will be difficult to avoid each other and a quick reconciliation is highly desirable. But think of the positives. Should you fall out of favour with your neighbours, it's very easy to move on. There are, of course, some downsides to a narrow boat home. Having to reverse yourself into the toilet, due to space limitations could, in time, become a little wearing but don't let that put you off. Tom Rolt himself, who lived aboard on his (seventy foot) narrow boat for several years was very proud of the fact that he had installed a bath with running hot water. He was very much the envy of all those around him, given that there were many homes at that time without such a facility. But living aboard is a very sustainable form of habitation with low energy needs as the water acts as an insulation material maintaining a relatively stable temperature within the boat.

After some time, the pair of Bratz dolls and their little friend needed a little more stimulation and were keen to know what the plans were. We decided it might be best to leave the boat here for now as it was a quiet spot and we would cycle back to the jeep.

'Can the Bratz girls come with us for a spin on the bike, Dad?' their friend and spokesperson enquires.

'Hmm, I'm not sure, have they any more suitable gear to wear?' I said, looking at their micro minis, stiletto heeled boots and full tee-shirts that were doing well to hold everything in without the added risk of physical exertion, 'have they any sort of old clothes, like for messing around outside?'

'Not really,' said my daughter while thinking, 'oh, Dad, what about cycling shorts and a bikini top?'

'The real job,' said I. Dolls these days are very poor role models for their impressionable companions. With figures to die for and the skimpiest of clothes it's little wonder that some children dress as they do.

There's an awful lot going on within the little heads of little people, of which we often have little conception. The bike ride to Vicarstown was very bumpy along a grass track – my passengers were in the child's seat on the back – and we nearly ended up in the canal on a couple of occasions. This detail did not go unnoticed by No 4.

'Dad, is there brakes on this bike?'

'There are – good brakes,' I reply with all the assurance of an air steward on a plummeting aircraft requesting the passengers to put on their life jackets.

'Dad is there brakes on a lawnmower?' asks the little voice from behind. I was puzzled by the question and had no idea where it was leading.

'Yeah, there are brakes on a ride-on lawnmower. Why do you ask?' I replied.

'Is there good brakes on our lawnmower?' The questioning was persistent.

'Course there's brakes on our mower,' I replied a bit testily, brought on by the repeated questioning and the physical effort required to propel us all along.

'And then how come you rode it into the pond last summer and you came in all soaking wet – remember? And you had to pull the lawnmower out with the jeep, remember?'

I remembered all right. It was time for us all to dismount and for me to push the bike. But for all of that, the bicycle is a relaxing way to travel along the canal. Modern mountain type bicycles are absolutely ideal for this purpose and the towpath provides a unique cycle path that is free from the hazards of road traffic. John Dunne's excellent guidebook, *Towpath Tours*, is an essential companion to take with you on a two-wheeled trip.

19. The Oil Fields

∞

It's seldom enough in life that business and pleasure meet. I do, of course, realise that the upper echelons of the business community claim that many of the real deals are cut on the golf course. This may be so but it's still hardly a good excuse to take up golf. But business and pleasure have, to a small degree, merged in my old roller-coaster of a life. There is actually a tenuous business link between my activities as a farmer and the inland waterways. If you suspect that this is simply a golfing-type sop to placate myself – and others – in defence of my leisure activities, then I will not disagree. Boating is, after all, a much more worthwhile activity than following a small ball in a pair of ridiculous shoes on very expensive turf. But I would prefer you to hear the arguments before you reach a conclusion.

I have for a long time been aware of the advantages of using renewable, plant-derived oils as a diesel replacement in boat engines. Most of us realise that diesel is a dangerous marine pollutant which is very toxic to all forms of aquatic life. Furthermore water is spoiled for human consumption with the slightest trace of diesel contamination.

Given that most of our municipal water supplies are drawn from rivers and lakes the potential for water contamination from inland craft is reasonably high. It's all too easy to inadvertently spill diesel into the water while refuelling the boat. A gust of wind or a shaky hand sends a good splash of oil into the water. And while you may nonchalantly ignore such a mishap, a rainbow coloured mess gathers around your boat in a very incriminating and embarrassing manner. Bilge pumps, in most cases, indiscriminately pump out all spilled oils from the engine bay into the water. It's reasonably obvious that diesel oil and the inland waterways don't mix. The environmental risks are becoming unacceptably high.

There is, of course, a much greater environmental dimension attached to the energy debate. Burning any carbon derived fuel such as oil, gas or coal, releases greenhouse gases, of which the most important is carbon dioxide. It is interesting to note that there is little new in the recognition of the greenhouse gas phenomena. The Victorians were aware that the massive amounts of carbon dioxide belting out of their great industrial chimneys could cause a blanket affect around the earth. It was none other than a Co. Carlow born physicist who first noted that atmospheric emissions of carbon dioxide and water acted as a radiation barrier trapping the earth's heat. In 1820 John Tyndall was born on the banks of the Barrow, in Leighlinbridge, and he was to become one of the greatest scientists of the nineteenth century. In 1859 Tyndall began a study of the properties of the main atmospheric gases and later concluded that carbon dioxide, water vapour and ozone had the ability to absorb heat radiation to a greater degree than the rest of the atmosphere. But Tyndall's experiments, in this field, were given scant regard at that time. This was, after all, the golden age of the railway and of huge industrial growth. The great manufacturing cities of Northern England were enveloped in a perpetual shroud of smog and fumes. Such was the Victorian's proficiency at air pollution one wonders why the ice caps didn't start dripping then. For example on the construction of the Manchester Ship Canal in the 1890s, coal usage for excavation and the transport of material peaked at a colossal 10,000 tonnes per day. Tyndall's precautionary and prophetic observations then, against the background of heavy Victorian industry, equates to the similar derision which the huge Chinese industries accord to the Kyoto Protocol today. The parallel doesn't end there. In the mid 1800s Britain was the Workshop of the World, a title that would be very appropriate to China today.

However, I don't entirely accept that the release of greenhouse gases is, by any means, the sole cause of global warming today. I am more of the view that the world's climate is continually in a state of change to a greater or lesser extent. Weather is very cyclical and it has been entirely consistent in this regard. It's quite ridiculous to attribute every flood and heat wave today to global warming – weather extremes have always happened and there are countless examples since records began. At the moment, some parts of the world are becoming warmer more quickly than the boffins expected. But I don't get too carried away with what a lot of these people think. There are vested interests on either side of this contentious argument. Scientific measurement of climate change has become much more accurate than heretofore and so trends can now be charted where no previous records existed. Sea levels are certainly rising – the Dutch, who have good reason to be concerned about such matters, are raising the dykes – but the seas rose up before with no input from man, whatsoever. I have in my garden a fossilised undersea rock removed from a hilltop on the farm which is evidence enough for me that water levels were extremely high, around here, a few million years ago.

I am of the view that we have a better chance of discovering oil in Offaly or eliminating Monday mornings than we have of significantly retarding global warming. However, neither am I naïve enough to believe that burning fossil fuels has nothing to do with global warming; on balance there is now ample evidence to concur with Tyndall's discovery that the greenhouse gas complex has an adverse effect on climate change. But whatever your view, the overriding factor in all of this must be; that at today's rate of consumption of the World's finite energy reserves and its resources of water and mineral wealth, human life cannot be sustained indefinitely. With the World's population trebling within the last eighty years and continuing to grow at a phenomenal rate, the human race certainly has the ability to suck the planet completely dry in a relatively short period of time.

The sum of all these factors would strongly suggest that we need to invoke a much more responsible environmental approach in all our human activities, whether work or pleasure. It seems reasonable to me that we should take a more discerning look at our pleasure pursuits in particular. Surface travel by ship and train, for passengers and goods, is hugely preferable from an environmental point of view to air travel depositing great carbon trails across Tyndall's blue sky. Nearer to home, I think it is reasonable for boating people to question their consciousness about the appropriateness of large engine pleasure craft on the inland waterways. There are plenty of cruisers out there on the Shannon with a pair of six cylinder diesels which wouldn't be out of place in a deep sea trawler or large earthmover. Smaller craft – which certainly includes narrow boats – tend to be much more meagrely powered.

Biofuels, whether in solid, liquid or gaseous form are those that are produced from living renewable resources and are now the buzz word. For power generation there are, for example, a plethora of fast growing woody crops and by-products that can be efficiently combusted to provide electrical energy. For the world of transport there are several options, some as old as time itself and others as new as a baby. Thus a horse drawn barge is an example of the early application of biofuels in transport. The horse's motive energy to tow the boat was derived from the consumption of rolled oats from its nosebag; thus oats was probably the first biofuel for transport. A contemporary example is an articulated truck fuelled on pure plant oil (PPO). PPO can be derived from a number of renewable resources such as waste (recovered) vegetable oil or the oilseed rape plant. With a little modification to the fuel system these oils can be used in what is an otherwise conventional diesel engine. It's not a new concept, though. The very first compression ignition engines were built to run on peanut oil by a brilliant German engineer by the name of Rudolf Diesel. Later on, with further developments in oil refining, the diesel engine was born. And now over a hundred years later, the wheel has gone full circle and vegetable oils are back in vogue.

However it should be understood that these alternative biofuels, will not be anything like sufficient to power the planet in a post fossil fuel era. Biofuels are not the panacea for all ills nor will they be the salvation of the World. There is quite simply not enough agricultural land available to feed the rapidly expanding world and, additionally, to produce energy crops. Increasing affluence in China and other parts of the new industrial world has pushed demands for wheat and rice to unprecedented levels. The quest for increased agricultural land to produce food and energy has become intertwined in a manner that, ironically, poses a new threat to the environment. Rain forests are now being cleared with a new zeal not seen since the Indians were pushed off the Great Plains. The livelihood of subsidence farmers is being threatened in a similar manner. Massive swathes of South America are being planted to sugar cane for ethanol production. Lucrative markets for exported grains can result in food becoming unobtainable for the indigenous population in poorer developing countries, not unlike in the early years of the Great Famine in Ireland. It is staggering the way circumstances can change in a very short period of time. Just five or so years ago, the developed world was awash with food and commodity prices were very low. Farmers, myself included, in Europe and North America were paid to put land into non food producing set-aside.

If I may use an example from our own farm to illustrate the competition that exists between energy crop and food production; we would have to plant one seventh of our farm area into the oilseed rape crop just to satisfy our own oil requirements alone. This, leaving aside the (currently) dubious economics, is unlikely to be a prudent use of land resources. Moreover, the energy ratio for this crop is not brilliant, at approximately one unit of energy in for every two out. But nationally biofuels will undoubtedly help to reduce our dependence on fossil fuels and their single greatest advantage is that they are carbon neutral. Neither is there one single solution; it will be the sum of a multitude of sources of alternative energy that will ultimately keep the wheels of society turning. I have no doubt that man's inventive ingenuity will rise admirably to the challenge of deriving energy from the most unforeseen and indeed much more obvious sources. The possibilities for wave/tidal-generated energy must be absolutely huge. It now appears quite extraordinary that such a source of potential power has remained untapped for so long. The abundance of cheap coal and oil over the last century simply ensured that brilliant minds were not challenged to explore other options.

In the light of all these escalating energy demands and developments, the Irish Department of Transport in 2007 funded a pilot project to convert a selection of road vehicles to run on PPO. While, technically, *The Tom Rolt* is far from a road vehicle, the powers-that-be were sufficiently convinced by the merits of my application to grant aid the conversion of my boat. Thus *The Tom Rolt* became the first boat – so far as I am aware – to be fuelled on PPO in this country, if not further afield.

It is also a project that I feel sure that the boat's namesake, the great Tom Rolt himself would have approved of. In his early life he was involved with some pioneering development work on diesel engines. Some of this work led to his one and only patent application which was a system to reduce the amount of black smoke emitted from diesel engines under load. However, it transpired that he was piped at the post by none other than the prestigious Daimler Company.

The conversion work to *The Tom Rolt's* engine was carried out by specialists in this new business on a showery day in late July, shortly after my return to Lowtown. It was not without a touch of irony that I had to rush home from the conversion work to start the harvest of the oilseed rape crop. Once this vulnerable crop is ready to fall to the knife, it becomes an absolute priority. The pods containing the tiny black oil-rich seeds can shed their precious burden with so little as a sneeze. Once the combine harvester was working in the field, within a very short time there was sufficient raw material harvested to power *The Tom Rolt* for an entire season of sustainable and environmentally sound boating on the inland waterways.

20. The End of the Line

⚭

With *The Tom Rolt* tanked up with pure plant oil, I eagerly awaited the first opportunity to slip off from a busy seasonal workload, on the inaugural trip. Despite broken weather for much of the harvest, matters were well wrapped up by the second weekend in September. We would travel on the boat up to Sallins and perhaps Naas, depending on how everything worked out. A volunteer crew was assembled without too much difficulty, namely my son and youngest daughter (No. 4).

The sun was pleasantly warm on our faces as we passed through the 19th lock at Lowtown. With plenty of time to spare, we moored in Robertstown to buy a few essentials. We had come to be fairly regular customers of the small supermarket there and for good reason. The deli counter is usually staffed by a young man who has to be Ireland's most pleasant shop assistant. Now I must confess that I am barely qualified to speak on such matters – not being a frequent shopper, simply because I dislike shopping. While I would hate to portray myself as sexist male, in truth shopping is for me, the same as cooking. I can only resort to either of these tasks if there isn't another option. But I have the greatest admiration for those who are expert at these essential activities. My ability to cook is very similar to my inept musical ability; I actually love watching television cookery programmes presented by people like Rachel Allen or Nigella Lawson but it would take at least a year of dedicated one-to-one tuition on a tropical island with either of these ladies before I'd have even mastered the basics.

This jolly chap, in Robertstown, is the perfect introduction to the shopping experience and is a pleasure to do business with. He helps me feel comfortable as I stupidly walk past the teabags for the tenth time and then still have to ask where they are. He's always welcoming, patient and efficient. There are many shop assistants in my limited experience, who have none of these qualities and couldn't care less about you or anyone else. It's a refreshing change to meet someone who actually likes their job. However my nominee for 'Shop Person of the Year' will eventually be lost from the retail industry as he's studying mechanical engineering.

Robertstown is an unspoilt village that has retained much of its character. The old Grand Canal Hotel is imposing in its dereliction but a full restoration would be wonderful. The village experienced something of a revival in the 1970s largely due to the efforts of local curate, Rev P. J. Murphy. However these efforts came to a sudden end with his untimely and tragic death following a traffic accident. Cruisers and canal boats have been hired from here in the recent past but this too has ceased. But no visit to Robertstown would be complete without partaking of a creamy pint of Guinness in the *Charlie Weld, a* very atmospheric canal public house. This great old establishment has been slaking the thirsts of canal folk and others since 1850.

Leaving the village the canal is carried on an embankment across what had proved to be very inhospitable and difficult terrain for the canal engineers. The Bog of Moods subsided with their early efforts – giving them a foretaste of what was to come as they traversed the

Great Bog of Allen – and as a result we have this arrow straight and raised embankment today. The closed Blackwood Feeder enters the canal at the end of this reach. This was once a navigable canal for approximately 5 km, whereby turf boats travelled into the bog to load at the turf banks during the Second World War. Like the nearby Milltown Feeder, it has an interesting history and I resolved to explore it on foot at a later date.

Departing the 18th lock, the surrounding countryside is in stark contrast to that below Lowtown on the Shannon Line. The farmland is rich and gently undulating with lots of expensive horse flesh galloping around the neatly stud railed fields. This countryside is the pulsing heart of the Irish bloodstock industry but since my equine experiences are limited to a contrary childhood Shetland pony, I am no expert. The 17th lock at Landenstown is a tidy and attractive place with a well-maintained former lock-keeper's cottage and a road bridge crossing the chamber to the entrance of a country house. Practically without exception all of these old cottages are very charming and desirable places to live. Graced with the elegance in miniature of much larger and grander houses, they are a design classic. With their waterside location and a few blooming herbaceous flowers lazily nodding their heads nearby, they paint an idyllic scene of picture postcard beauty.

After Digby Bridge the canal makes a sharp bend to our right. There is an interesting reason for this sudden change in direction. The original engineer for the Grand Canal, the Dutchman Thomas Omer, had intended to lock down into the River Liffey, which is straight ahead, and lock up the opposite side. The River Barrow, at Monasterevin, was traversed in this laborious manner for a few years, prior to the building of that aqueduct. But when the English engineers, John Smeaton and William Jessop were over to sort out a lot of the early construction problems they took a different view. Omer's plans were given a short shift, principally due to the wastage of canal water to the Liffey. A pair of double locks on either side of the river would also have greatly increased travelling time. Thus it was agreed, at the eleventh hour to build an aqueduct to cross the river but not at the site of Omer's intended locks on which work had already begun. Thus the canal excavation was swung sharply to traverse the river with the aqueduct, situated further upstream at the site of an old ford.

The Leinster Aqueduct, which dates from 1780, is the result of all this controversy and is an imposing structure of five arches with the parapet walls terminating in attractive round stone pillars. We moored *The Tom Rolt* in its channel to scramble down the embankment to the river below. There is a mysterious rural beauty to the Liffey here – in contrast to most people's perception of this river – as it follows a very twisted secluded path. Perhaps as a result of this perception, I had anticipated that the aqueduct might be a very grand structure on a par with the Boyne Aqueduct on the Royal Canal but they share little in common. The Leinster Aqueduct is wider and probably longer but the Boyne Aqueduct is much more elevated which bestows it with a greater sense of engineering excellence. Since the closure of the Blackwood reservoir, it became necessary to have an auxiliary water supply for the Grand Canal and water can be pumped up here from the river below. While these pumps are a relatively recent installation and are electrically powered, steam pumps were commonly used for this purpose in England. As long ago as 1784, a Watt beam engine pumped water up into the Birmingham Canal. The earliest application of steam power was, in fact, for pumping water, typically out of coal mines.

Shortly after the Liffey crossing the canal traveller is faced with a dilemma at the Soldiers Island's junction, of either a left turn for Sallins or right for Naas. Interestingly, the Naas branch line ascends from the main line here up to its own summit level. As nightfall was becoming ever closer we decided to strike for Sallins not least, to take on some provisions for the evening meal. The route is pleasantly twisted around here if one had plenty of time to enjoy it but its interest was lost on me as the sun was rapidly sinking into a great red ball. But the pressures of time have, thankfully, little bearing on children and No. 4 saw the opportunity to break into song with a slight reworking of a popular classic. Using the knot on the end of the bow rope as a microphone she sang out;

'Is this the way to Sallins (Amarillo), Sal a la la lala,' to the tune of the old Neil Sedaka number. It surely was, as the suburbs of the town were quickly in sight. We moored close to the mill and went ashore.

Sallins has a proud industrial heritage. In the 1840s a well documented stand-off arose here, whereby the Grand Canal Company refused permission to the GSWR to build a bridge crossing over the canal. But this was as futile an effort as that of old King Canute himself to thwart the inevitable progress of the railways and the Grand Canal Company were forced to concede. At the time of the First World War, a sugar beet factory was built just outside of the town but in common with the much earlier plant in Mountmellick, its days were short lived. However it is more notable as one of the first buildings in Ireland constructed with reinforced mass concrete, although Portland cement has been around for over 150 years. Close by, a meat factory was built on the site of the former Grand Canal Hotel which had been demolished in a 1960s act of heritage vandalism.

I had a memorable experience here – for all the wrong reasons – in the former meat factory, about twenty years ago. Reversing a livestock trailer laden with a casualty animal up to a small doorway on a dark November night, the rear offhand corner of the jeep collided with a parked articulated trailer. I quickly jumped out, surveyed the damage and then proceeded to challenge the man who was supposed to be directing me safely back.

'How come,' I said, quite irately as I (very) occasionally can become, 'that you wouldn't tell me to stop before I reversed into the trailer?'

'Cos, you weren't back far enough. I told you to back up close to the door,' he gruffly replied, his blood stained apron emphasising the size of his huge belly. His massive bare arms were covered in tattoos all the way up to his shoulders. His great neck was akin in its mass to that of his bovine victims, with a couple of folds of overlapping skin where it merged into his shoulders.

I thought he was a miserable so-and-so but I didn't articulate this view as it's not wise to argue with a butcher in a meat factory. I could have, very easily, ended up in slices floating down the canal.

The mill is on the opposite bank to the old meat factory. But unlike practically all the old mills along the Barrow, this is very much a modern working example. Formerly owned by the Quaker milling family, W. P. & R. Odlum, this renowned brand name is now part of the industry leading IAWS group of companies. The Odlum family opened their first mill in Maryborough (now Portlaoise) in 1845 and by the end of the 1920s were operating a total of nine mills. Eventually in line with the rest of the industry, all the smaller and less efficient mills were closed with just the three large flour mills in Dublin, Cork and Portarlington left remaining. All of these mills have been upgraded and the Odlum Group is now the largest flour miller in Ireland with at least 50% of the domestic market. Approximately one third of their wheat needs are sourced on the Irish market with the balance imported. The Sallins plant is home to a dedicated oatmeal milling facility which produces porridge and other oaten products for both the domestic and export markets.

It is encouraging to note that while, almost without exception, none of the old milling families are still involved, the Irish flour milling and baking industry is in relatively good shape. The despondency that I experienced passing the old Barrow mills is mitigated to a fair degree by the incredible success of Irish food companies such as IAWS. With innovative product development such as their Cuisine de France brand, the consumption of bread and freshly baked speciality products has become fashionable again. It is also a fact that the Irish flour milling industry has now a larger share of the domestic flour market than it had one hundred years ago. The old order has certainly changed but the flour and baking industries are, in truth, probably the stronger for it. And whether we like it or not, there has been one continuous and simple thread throughout this tale of waterside mills; price competition from imported product ensures only those who react positively to competition and become leaner and fitter can hope to survive. Customer loyalty and traditional practice counts for nothing. However, I feel duty bound to record that, more often than not, farmers are the businesses who can stand to lose most from these import pressures. Farmers are primary producers to whom the phrase 'added value' has sadly little meaning. While I may run my own farm business in as ultra efficient manner as is possible, many of the exporting competitor countries have inherent production advantages that we can only dream about.

With our shopping needs met in Sallins, we walked down to the quay below the bridge. Here there are a diverse range of boats moored, some of which seem to be live-a-boards, all of which creates a pleasant sense of a vibrant canal community. A few miles further downstream, the small village of Hazelhatch is the undisputed centre for live-a-board canal boats in Ireland. To walk along the canal bank there is to experience all sorts of floating homes with permanently integrated services suggestive of being what boaters refer to as olympic flames – which is a boat that never goes out. But one gets the sense that it is quite a close set community into which it may take the newcomer sometime to become integrated.

We considered staying put in Sallins for the night but as the vision of that cleaver bearing butcher was too vividly refreshed in my mind, we turned the boat for home in search of a more secluded spot. Passing the small wooded Soldiers Island at the three-legged canal junction, I thought that this would be a novel – and indeed safe –

place to moor.

'Hey, what do you think, will we pull in here?' I shouted to the bo'sun who was immersed in a *Top Gear* magazine up in the saloon. The stove was lit and the cabin lights were on. It looked really cosy down there and as there were few creature comforts at the Captain's post, I couldn't wait to moor for the night.

'What's that you said, Dad? I can't hear you over the roar of the twin Cat V8s,' came back the reply. My son was poking fun at our Kubota engine. As a young lad he was taken on a trip on a Severn class RNLI lifeboat which was powered by a pair of Caterpillar eight cylinder engines.

'Will I pull in here, along the island and under those trees?' I questioned.

'No, don't. That place is full of rats and it's probably haunted with some auld soldier hangin' around for the last couple of hundred years for a boat just like yours to stop here for the night.'

With no wish to make this spectre's night, I quickly moved away. Just then and right on cue, a big brown rat dived off the island bank and into the canal beside us. Whatever about the ghostly soldier, the bo'sun was right about the rats. I don't know how he knew.

I throttled up the plant oil fuelled engine – which was going like a treat with only the slightest hint of frying chips noticeable when within the confines of a lock – and turned towards the aqueduct and Lowtown. There was a light breeze blowing down the boat which carried the gorgeous aroma of wood smoke. It is a wonderfully evocative smell that reminds me of happy childhood winter evenings coming indoors all drippy-nosed and rosy-cheeked to the warmth of a log fire. But by the same token, the smell of coal smoke spiralling from city chimneys, a memory from my teenage years, is a less than happy one. For part of my education I was sent to a boarding school in Dublin, which I actively disliked. I will forever associate the smell of coal smoke with returning to the school on cold winter Sunday nights when the Georgian grates of Dublin 4 were well stoked up with coal. But the school building itself was almost devoid of heat save for a few miserly old storage heaters. We frequently awoke to ice on the insides of the great old rattling dormitory sash windows. The more sickly scent of turf smoke carries much more neutral memories. It is very much a smell of winter on the Grand Canal and its heartland towns of Allenwood, Edenderry and Tullamore. But I suspect that there was also a coal burning fraternity within the merchant class of Tullamore, who felt that turf was the fuel of the working man.

We moored for the night below the 16th lock at Digby Bridge. This is the only jetty serving the three locks between Robertstown and Sallins which is a poor show for Waterways Ireland. I switched off the engine, well satisfied with its first full day's performance on renewable oil. It seemed right and proper to be fuelled on a natural product that was in total harmony with the richly bio-diverse environment around us. But the real bonus of the conversion was immediately obvious as I ducked my head down to enter the cabin below. Gone forever was the awful cloying smell of diesel, replaced with the homely and ever so subtle smell of hot chip oil. It was nothing like the smell of a greasy Joe's type of chipper – which in many ways would be fine – but much more Mc Donalds, almost verging on the up market Eddie Rocket's. It gave me a great sense of achievement and furthermore, all of my old engine bugbears had been addressed.

I walked up to the bridge and listened pensively to the gurgle of excited water leaking through the sluices. Water has an innate and insatiable desire for escape and abhors quiet containment; it is forever restless, plagued by the perpetual pull of gravity. I sat down quietly on the balance beam – it was damp and cold in the autumnal night air. The hedgerow birds were chirping their last shrill and startled calls, all too aware that warm early autumn days would soon be increasingly few and far between. I looked down at our little home on the water, its humble yellow light reflected on the still water. The smoke from the chimney was in an upward bound shaft with a slight bias to the way in which we had come. I could no longer smell its enchanting aroma. Life can have its absolute memorable moments, some good and others much less so. This evening time was one of life's quietly reassuring and sacred little intervals; a busy autumn in the fields lay ahead but the stress of a difficult harvest was over for another year.

After a good night's sleep for some and a more fitful one for others, we woke to a lovely misty and cool September morning. With a quick and refreshing wash in the waters of the canal, we left for a pre breakfast stroll up to the bridge and lock. There appears to have been a side chamber here but for what reason I do not know. The road was unusually quiet with only the occasional vehicle to disturb the very subdued and peaceful setting. We returned to the boat after a short while to begin preparations for a hearty breakfast that would sustain us throughout most of the day. With the meal over and the living area well tidied up – order and good housekeeping are very important when space is limited – we started the engine and cast off. The canal is very wide at this point but since our first trip the banks have been cleared of overhanging bushes and branches. While the seclusion that such overhanging vegetation offers is pleasant, an occasional clean up along the banks is very necessary.

It was a very enjoyable return trip on that Sunday morning. The sun gently warmed us up as I stood with my hand on the tiller, idly watching the human and animal life go about their morning chores and routines. Finches darted nervously from bush to bush while the occasional car passed by with steamy windows full of yawning children who gaped enviously as they were shepherded off to church. An old buck rabbit paused quizzically to consider our passing. Those greedy old scavengers of the skies – the crows – circled over a distant stubble field, now with the harvest gathered forced to work a little more honestly for their keep. Crows and wasps and slugs are my three less favourite creatures – what the Good Lord was thinking about when he created this loathsome trio, I can't fathom. Perhaps He was feeling a little disgruntled with the carry-on of Adam and Eve in the harmonious Garden of Eden and created a few wasps to keep them away from the ripe fruit. But such uncharitable personal feelings towards other forms of creation were not warranted or desirable on this beautiful Sunday morning. There is never a repetitive air about retracing one's steps on the canal; this is an ever changing environment and at our speed of travel there is always something new or different to see.

Of all the senses, the sight of our eyes is our greatest asset – it is the one that I most treasure. I am becoming increasingly conscious that I all too often fail to use my eyes to their best effect. There is so much to see in the world around us and yet all too often, little of it seems to register with us. It's sometimes necessary to make a conscious effort to see more around us. We take the familiar for granted failing to observe the small subtle changes in the environment as the season progresses. The living, changing and unfolding vista before us on the canal that morning was a case in point. If an adult – children could be forgiven – became indifferent or fed up with such a mode of travel, the failing would be his. But unfortunately people do become worn and weary with life and for many of us it is part of our very nature. Sometimes we become so blinkered and introspective that it is difficult to see beauty or peace, in the place or people that surround us. In this respect the canal is, for me, an unfailing place for silent and rewarding reflection.

* * * * * * * *

I made my first visit to The Blackwood Reservoir – or Ballynafagh Lake as it is alternatively known – on a fine morning in mid December. This man-made lake is located in a bog close to the source of the River

IN THE WAKE OF GIANTS

Slate, where there are several springs in the area. This great reservoir was constructed by William Jessop as an auxiliary water supply, in addition to the Milltown Feeder, to the summit level of the Grand Canal. The aforementioned Dutch Engineer, Thomas Omer, had planned to use the Liffey tributary, the Morrell, as the sole feeder to his planned lower summit level. But Smeaton and Jessop had much more ambitious plans which were ultimately implemented. However the feeder canal which is 5 km long was closed in the 1950s but remained navigable for a few years thereafter. The water level in the reservoir was also intentionally lowered and eventually the canal bed was drained and partially filled in.

The countryside had regressed into bogland as I left the main road and drove down a tarred cul-de-sac. This had deteriorated into a rough and potholed lane by the time it reached the last house. Leaving my vehicle, I walked along a scrubby track, hopeful that it would lead me to the water. In the near distance I could see a ruined building and a raised embankment that might well surround the man-made lake. My expectation was positively confirmed; this was indeed what I was looking for and the small building was the remains of the former sluice-keeper's cottage. This was straddling the stone culvert underneath drawing water from the lake. Apparently the keeper was able to operate the sluice in the culvert below his tiny house without having to venture outside. But I could see no evidence of this as the original sluices had been replaced with large Victorian cast iron gate valves. The water flow from the lake had, laterally, been controlled by adjusting these.

I scrambled excitedly down to the beautifully arched culvert opening. There was a mere trickle of water flowing out of the stone lined tunnel which bore water marks high up on its side walls. Much to my delight I discovered that the keystone of the little arch was dated. It was built exactly 220 years before my visit, in the year 1787. I peered down the arrow straight and arched tunnel which has three stones in perfectly horizontal lines on either side of the keystone for its entire length. While this is, in many ways, a very simple stone structure, it is nonetheless, a beautifully executed example of the stonemason's art. It's the quality of workmanship that makes such a construction so different to anything of similar purpose that would be built today. As you travel along a motorway it's likely that you will cross a culvert of this size every few hundred metres. But the culverts of today are simply big precast concrete pipes that are placed in an open trench with a laser-levelled excavator. It takes a few hours and the job is completed with a low level of skill. I don't doubt that this is, of course, welcome and necessary progress. But the point I wish to emphasise is that for excellence in engineering and beautifully accurate workmanship, carefully built to last centuries, such canal stonework remains unsurpassed.

I walked up on the surrounding embankment expecting to see a large body of water. But the reservoir level has been allowed to fall by the opening of a drain on the other side of the lake. Through years of neglect the embankment has become broken down and the lake size has been reduced to a shadow of its former self. I could see open water out towards the middle of the lake and the foreground was a wetland dominated with rushes, reeds, sedges and reed mace. But for all of that it was a very beauteous scene. The water plants were in their winter senesced colours of shades of yellow and brown and every colour variation in between. The bogland surrounding the wetlands was covered in heathers and brackens and some gorse, all in their winter clothes. Interspersed along the bank where the peaty soil yielded to the marshes were the trees who like their roots sipping the water; birch, alder and willow. Further up on the higher ground a few hawthorn and ash seemed to prosper. In the far distance the tower of the ruined Ballynafagh church adds an eloquent dimension of rural tranquillity to the landscape.

In an effort to become closer to the open water, I followed a grassy path, worn enough by solitary walkers to be free of heather and bracken which trailed along the top of the old embankment. From this unfolding vantage point it was possible to see the extent of the former reservoir. I do not know what area it encompasses but is a substantial area of perhaps twelve or more acres. It was truly a massive construction project, whereby the clay had to be carted into the bog to build this great surrounding wall to contain the water within. It is estimated that it may have held close to half a million tonnes of water when it was full. This colossal amount of stored water would have exerted truly phenomenal forces on the containing clay wall. And such a wall is only as strong as its weakest build. If the water detected the slightest weakness, all its latent energy would be cruelly concentrated on the flaw and within a very short time the smallest escaping rivulet would become a raging stream drying out the great reservoir.

As I walked in an easterly direction following the old path, the open water became gradually more into view. I became hopeful that I might be led to the water's very edge by one of the little weaving tangential paths. Following one of these trails through some scrubby wetland trees, I suddenly found myself – much to my delight – at the open water. It was crystal clear right down to its peaty bottom. Three swans were feeding further out, but sufficiently curious, they headed my way. The low winter sun was diminished by gathering grey and sinister clouds. The stillness had succumbed to a very slight breeze; the weather was about to change. The light that had been so kind to this area of outstanding natural beauty was fading rapidly. I had been very privileged by circumstances outside of my control that allowed me to find this place when I did. Suddenly it struck me as rather strange that this surreal and completely unspoilt piece of God's earth was created with the help of man.

I knelt down on the bank and cupping my hands, scooped up some water to drink. My mind returned as to how I had come to be here, immersed in such a place. The beauty of the canal had led me to its source; perhaps of life itself.

Epilogue

⋧

O n a misty early winter's day, we were driving through rural Gloucestershire, in the south west of England, bound for the little hamlet of Stanley Pontlarge. The weak winter sun was making a gallant effort to break through the still greyness, but with only fleeting success. The trees still bore some frail remnants of their autumn leaves, enough to suggest that it had been a beautiful season. The more open and dreary countryside around Bristol, had given way to a gently undulating and more wooded country. In time the beautiful yellow sandstone buildings so typical of the Cotswolds became gradually more prevalent. It seems to me that this picture postcard tract of middle England has remained relatively unspoilt by the demands of urban and industrial society.

Without much difficulty we found our destination and turned in a narrow lane guided by an old sloping black and white finger-post sign. A Victorian iron railway bridge crossed over our heads as the sandstone gable end of a house came into view, which Peter, my brother-in-law, instantly recognised. He had been here before, many years ago. I was almost trembling with excitement; the picture that I had painted in my mind's eye of the setting of the great man's house was reasonably accurate. In the final book of his autobiographical trilogy, Tom Rolt devotes a descriptive chapter to his ancient home. A young child about to enter Santa's grotto for the first time could not have rivalled my sense of anticipation.

We opened the small wooden pedestrian gate at the gable end; the house has its back to the lane. Nothing short of a magical and very picturesque scene lay in front of us as we rounded the corner and came into the front garden. A low dry stone wall surrounded the lawn, with its sleeping rose beds and an elderly pear orchard lying outside the boundary hedge. An old stone garden shed lay in the far corner. The house is known as The Cottage, which gives a false impression of what to expect, not so much in its prettiness, but in its size. The charming house is in two parts, one larger and greatly older than the other. The main building's origins lie in medieval times when it was built as a courthouse under the ancient manorial system and dates from the fourteenth century. The smaller part of the house is more recent and dates from the eighteenth century. The tiny, almost copper green and roughly cut roof slates are quite the oldest and prettiest I have ever seen. This ancient house, not least its sagging roof, required attention when Rolt returned to live here after his father's death. A local builder, advised him to be done with the troublesome slipping slates and replace them with concrete tiles. He had profoundly misjudged his client; the roof was lovingly stripped and repaired and all of the original slates went back on.

We entered through a low doorway into the kitchen complete with beams and uneven stone flags and a pine table spread with an indoor picnic lunch. An old range cooker added to the cosy and relaxed atmosphere.

Sonia Rolt is an absolutely amazing person. With a sprightliness and sharpness of mind that would put many a person half her age to shame, she is a most engaging lady. A widow since 1974, she has devoted a great part of her life to perpetuating the pioneering work of her husband. A frequent speaker on matters of industrial archaeology and an acknowledged expert on English canals, it is as a result of her efforts that there are eight of her late husband's books currently in print. This is an incredible achievement given that many of these books were first published over fifty years ago.

I take away one very abiding memory from this visit. Sonia Rolt, in her generous hospitality, insisted that we go upstairs to her late husband's study and view his collection of books. I followed in his well–worn footsteps up the twisted dark wooden staircase. His small study is on the corner of the house with an off-square window in each exterior wall. I could almost hear Tom tapping away on his old typewriter, the desk covered in open reference books, the air thick with cigarette smoke. The light outside was rapidly fading; the mist had thickened into a fog. We spoke of his many and less well known interests from philosophy to agriculture and to the supernatural. Leaving the study, we did as we were bidden and climbed up the little creaking stairway to the attic to view a further collection of his books and artefacts shelved amid the very ancient oak roof trusses. The electric light did not work but the closing daylight entering through the two dormer windows provided us with a quality of atmosphere that was almost surreal.

There are times in life when circumstances conspire to produce truly bizarre happenings. When time and place amalgamate in strange alliance to create that which is not natural. When forces beyond the control of man collaborate with split second timing. As we stood in the decaying and shadowed eerie light, the unmistakable sound of a steam locomotive crossed the damp night air. We looked at each other. The sound grew louder; there was no doubt. The mingled smells of burning coal, hot oil and hissing steam accompanied the clanking of steel on steel. The windows resonated with a reverence to the passing train. We watched her disappear off into the distance, the pall of smoke pausing briefly along the line, knowing that we had been extremely privileged.

While the rest of the world desired the obliteration of a great age of industrial heritage, Rolt cried stop. What finer tribute could we have witnessed to the pioneering canal and steam preservation work of the man who had lived here? I left Stanley Pontlarge happy in the knowledge that Tom Rolt could rest in peace beside the miniature but extraordinarily beautiful Norman church across from his former home, with only the occasional rumble of a steam locomotive to disturb his slumber.